The Secret Life of an Evangelical

Beth Dickson

For Neil
husband and friend

British Library Cataloguing in Publication Data
A catalogue record for this book is available from the British Library

ISBN 0-900128-33-X

Cover Design by Potion 9 Design
Typeset by A.R. Cross
Printed and bound in Great Britain
for Partnership
by Bell and Bain Ltd, Glasgow

Contents

Introduction

For me, the most important thing about life is that it provides an opportunity to know God. This 'knowledge' is about getting to know someone with whom you are in relationship, rather than knowing a set of facts. Everything that I learn about God occurs in the context of another set of relationships—those with fellow-Christians. I was brought up in a Christian Brethren church and still worship with a congregation which has its roots in that movement. That group belongs to a wider group within the church, commonly designated as Evangelicals who are orthodox in Christian belief but have a series of distinguishing features. They hold the Bible in special regard; they focus in their preaching on the cross of Christ; they believe that conversion opens the way to new life in Christ; and they actively promote their faith. Both these groups belong to the worldwide church. Sometimes these relationships are full of health and at other times they can be much more difficult. Whatever their nature, they are always the stuff of sanctification as God straightens out what is twisted and sheds light on what is dark.

I decided to write these reflections for a number of reasons. Firstly, the Christian Brethren have often been seen as intellectually primitive and tediously strict. Though I'm not their greatest fan, that isn't a fair judgement. They could be attractively enthusiastic and reflective too. Secondly, I have found that many things I have been interested in, have not been important in the local church nor for Evangelicals more generally. It has seemed to me that as an Evangelical I have had a secret life. This is an attempt to narrate the relationship between the individual and the church and to explore whether this secrecy is a necessity of belonging to an institution which cannot and should not be expected to mirror the intimacy of the relationship of the believer with God; or whether on the other hand, the church is ignoring areas of human life which, if acknowledged, would make churches seem more real.

At least that is what I thought I was trying to write about. Thinking over it now, I wonder if I haven't just been looking for God, more deeply, more determinedly, more hesitantly, more absorbingly, more desperately, right from the start. See what you think yourself.

Beth Dickson

CHAPTER 1

Conversion

The first spiritual reality of which I was explicitly aware was of my need to be 'saved'. I picked this up principally from Gospel meetings. My parents certainly did not make this expectation explicit and I do not remember my Sunday school teachers doing so either. But at the Gospel meetings—church services convened weekly on Sunday nights in order to explain to adults how they might become converted—I grasped that I was a 'sinner', there was a separation between me and God and that Jesus loved me so much that he came to die to take away my sins. By trusting in him I could be restored to fellowship with God. However, for a long time I felt rather diffident about my conversion story because most of the stories told in public were very dramatic.

Saul's Conversion

The most famous template for this experience, and one commonly referred to by Evangelicals, was that of the Apostle Paul. Originally named Saul, he was an intelligent, passionate Pharisee who understood very early on the nature and extent of the challenge which followers of Jesus of Nazareth posed to Judaism. His dynamic nature led him to condone the most violent measures in his attempt to root out the fledgling church. He watched as Stephen, an early church leader, was stoned to death. On his way to Damascus, in order to put an end to the Christians there, Saul was stopped in his tracks by a bright light from heaven and a voice saying, 'Saul, Saul, why are you persecuting me?' In reply to Saul's question about who was addressing him, the answer came, 'I am Jesus whom you are persecuting.' Saul was told to go to

Damascus and await instructions. He was blind for three days and did not eat or drink. Then Ananias, a local Christian, came and prayed with him. Saul received his sight (something like scales fell from his eyes, the Bible says) and was charged by God to take the good news about Jesus to the Gentile world at the cost, eventually, of his own life.

The experience revolutionised Saul's identity to the extent that he took a new name—Paul. In his encounter with God his whole life was laid bare and everything which he had been sure would find favour with God—his Jewishness, his Pharisaical training, the dedication of his natural abilities—had actually led him away from God. For someone who prided himself on his education and understanding, the three days of blindness were a profoundly ironic commentary on his previous beliefs about himself. Coupled with his experience of blindness was an outstanding experience of grace. Despite everything, God loved him and wanted to extend to him forgiveness and reconciliation in Jesus. Paul never got over that experience. It is described several times in Acts and also referred to in the epistles.

Evangelical Conversion

All Evangelicals know in their heads and in their hearts that it is at the cross that our relationship with God begins. It is there we discover the woeful mess and culpable muddle of our lives and the good news that Jesus, by his death and resurrection, is able to offer forgiveness for sins and reconciliation with God. Sometimes this realisation happens very obviously and quickly. This tremendous change, called conversion, is often described by the individual as a powerful experience of God. Apart from Paul, Evangelicals often look at turning points in the lives of great Christian leaders such as Augustine, Martin Luther, John Wesley and Charles Spurgeon and see a similar pattern. In Evangelical preaching it is common to preach for conversions—as the evangelist Billy Graham has. Many missions take place precisely in order to acquaint people with the rudiments of the Gospel and persuade them to trust in Christ. Thus the experience becomes widely replicated.

My Conversion

Of the conversion stories referred to within Evangelical preaching most are of the dramatic variety. However, not all converted people have a startling story of conversion: this is especially true of the children of believing parents. Brought up in a Christian family, I cannot remember a time when I did not know and love Jesus. Around the age of seven or eight, I realised that I could not rely on my parent's faith and must trust Christ for myself. This I did and was quite amazed by the depths of my parents' reaction. My dad spoke to me by myself—something quite unusual—and read me 1 Timothy 1.15 and then John 3.16 encouraging me to put my name into the verse when 'whosoever' turned up—these were Authorised Version days. This made complete sense to me and I realised that God loved me and wanted me to trust him. My dad seemed quite close to tears and so did my mum, which was strange. I cannot really say that I felt anything much except pleased that I had done something which had pleased my mum and dad. I could not see that there was anything to cry about—surely everybody would be happy now? I went off to bed to read an article in one of my books about the life of Beatrix Potter. Although I read for ages, I could not fall off to sleep and went back downstairs to explain this to my parents. They said that I was probably a bit over-excited and would soon fall asleep if I went back to bed. Anyway the next day was Monday and I would need to get up for school. They seemed quite normal again and, on going back to bed, I did eventually fall asleep. And Monday was very normal.

This 'conversion' story has to be one of the least dramatic in the history of Evangelicalism. I had no awareness of any supernatural presence, nor did I have any feelings other than those I was used to, although I did think my parents' behaviour was slightly unusual. For a long while I was quite embarrassed about this—it seemed so pathetic in comparison with the conversions I frequently heard about.

However, it was much more of a problem for the boys in the congregation because in the course of time they had to describe their conversions at church services known as 'testimony meetings'. These services were popular at New Year. Quite a few of the men who spoke had been converted in adult life and had often lived for a long time without the faintest thought of God in their heads. Their experiences had definite 'before' and 'after' elements in them. Boys, who were about fourteen or fifteen at this time, and had made a profession of faith during childhood, had to squeeze their experience into the conversion story shape with which they were familiar. This meant that mildly mischievous boyhood escapades had to be elevated to the status of 'sinful past' so that their conversion would appear to have some reality. Thus hours playing illegally around building-sites were equated with Paul's pre-Damascus experience. Even as a child I thought this comparison unlikely, and my insight was corroborated by my mother's laughter and my father's tut-tutting. I realised quite early on that Christians often interpret their lives by what they have been taught to expect, *whether or not it accords with reality.*

Conversion and Theology

Theology was not something that we in the Brethren were too interested in. We had Scripture and the Holy Spirit and quite piously—but incredibly arrogantly—we thought we had nothing to learn from people who had devoted their lives to the study of the revealed God. Thus the tension between what we believed about our lives and what happened to us continued. Our Christian lives were a round of church meetings and evangelistic activities which we were supposed to enjoy and be enthusiastic about. Nobody ever said they were boring—though I was often bored. Other pursuits, such as reading or sport, were not encouraged or not discussed but I spent vast amounts of time reading and watching television, often feeling that it was a cop-out and I should be doing something 'spiritual'.

Encountering Reformed theology at university did wonders for my view of sanctification. I did think that Christians should live good lives but that came a long way behind supporting the activities of the local assembly. The bracing blasts of Reformed theology, expressed through logical argument, were successful in demolishing the repetitive but content-free exhortation which made up a great deal of my teaching. I remember reading the chapter on sanctification in Sinclair Ferguson's *The Christian Life* and the scales fell from my own eyes when I realised how organically the righteous life related to the new birth. Borrowing the language of Saul's conversion indicates the dramatic turnaround in my worldview. Because I do not believe in a second conversion experience, I had no category into which to put this event. Looking at it from this distance, it does have 'conversion' elements about it: repentance is clear in the change of thinking and the change did take place very quickly. However, I had been a Christian for years so it was not the time when I passed from life to death, although it was a significant moment for me.

The Community Founded on Conversions

While I thought, and my tradition taught me to expect, that what happened to me, happened to every Christian, I was unaware how deeply my tradition had been influenced by the circumstances in which it was born. In Scotland, the Christian Brethren planted a number of new congregations in the wake of the revivals of 1859-60. During these years conversions were numerous as the Spirit called many into the Kingdom. Often those converted came from working-class backgrounds and, because of the lives they were turning away from, had classic conversion experiences. The conversion of local blacksmith, Richard Sharkey, in Kilmarnock in the 1860s was thought to be so dramatic it was written up as a short tract which was used in evangelism. This meant that at the meeting point between

Christianity and society the Brethren functioned like a large railway station where people travelling in the wrong direction in life were re-routed. The main concern of most Brethren churches was to enable people to repent and believe. The fact that there was life beyond the busy railway station—both in Christianity and society—was of little importance given the eternal significance of the task in hand.

However, the radical social changes which characterised the 1960s meant that society moved on and the message the Brethren had honed in order to communicate most successfully from the 1860s onwards was no longer understood by society. Ironically, while Marshall McLuhan was helpfully explaining that the medium was the message, the Brethren were just as stubbornly paying no attention. They could not separate the unchanging message from the media through which they had received it and, because the medium is the message *whether you like it or not*, what people heard was old-fashioned strictness in living which made no sense to the 60s hedonists. Brethren had found open-air preaching useful in communicating the Gospel. In the late-nineteenth century there was little to do in miners' rows and if an evangelist, gifted in communication, came along, they created a stir and found a ready audience. Television put an end to open-air preaching because it was more professionally entertaining and not so personally demanding. Brethren refused to accept this. Some Brethren were found holding an open-air meeting on a Sunday next to an office block which was empty. When asked why they did this, they replied that they had always come to this place—there used to be some houses there.

When I was beginning to ask questions about God, my tradition was being asked questions by God. Would it be realistic about its relationship with him, and move on into his future? However, many interposed the tradition between themselves and God and refused to believe that God would work in new ways. We were living in 'days of declension and departure'. What was so deeply upsetting about all this was that the refusal to accept reality became a refusal to accept God. This refusal polarised the movement as some churches stayed true to the evangelistic spirit of the tradition, and began to innovate in order to keep the lines of communication with society open so that by whatever means the Gospel could be preached. Other churches, although appearing to preserve the tradition in externals, strayed from its life and went into full-scale religious retreat. My personal experience of an undramatic conversion in a tradition which expected dramatic conversions was a tiny symptom of a much larger inability to face reality experienced by an entire network of churches. Although the expectations of dramatic conversions only resulted in some minor embarrassment for me, the belief that Gospel preachers should not even take minimal responsibility for ensuring that their message was 'heard' was catastrophic.

The Peter Rabbit Conversion

The psalmists constantly encourage people to remember how God has worked in their lives. They are aware that people need to practise looking for God or listening to him for, unless he reveals himself in his 'all-singing, all-dancing' mode, we are quick to assume he is not with us. Nobody said worshipping an invisible God was easy. Looking back to the night when I told my parents I wanted to follow Jesus, I wrote that I had no sense of the supernatural—and that was true enough. However, that absolutely and categorically does not mean that God was absent. All it means is that he was invisible. Into the life of a child he was drawing to himself he had placed two human beings, a mother and a father, precisely to further this purpose. They created a home in which he was worshipped and where his stories and his ways were taught. Even though the family's expectations of how the child should respond to God might seem odd to some, they too were of use. Just as he had planned, when her understanding had matured enough, he called her in a voice, familiar since conception and no less authoritative for not being audible; and she came. No drama. But God taking infinite pains and working in the life of what? A mere child, and a girl at that, with no status of any sort, from a town few people had ever heard of. And yet that child was called in a way she understood, in a family context which made sense to her and in a way which hinted at how her life would develop. No wonder her parents were moved by the occasion.

It is interesting to me now, looking back, as a person who has spent much of her professional life working with fiction, that fiction too should be a part of this experience. Probably my understanding of sin was about as deep as Peter Rabbit's knowledge that he should not trespass into Mr McGregor's garden. Probably, like Peter, I could have done with some camomile tea after the evening's excitement. Definitely God is as interested in children and as keen to communicate with them as he is to engage the attention of rampaging Pharisees. It would be surprising if he used the same methods.

CHAPTER 2

On the Un/happiness of Women and the Kindness of Men

I made up my first evangelistic sermon before I was seven. I probably didn't know the word 'sermon' because we didn't use it—we spoke of the preacher's 'message'—and I certainly didn't know the word 'evangelistic'. (I can only date the memory roughly—it occurred in the first house my family lived in and we moved when I was seven.) However, I knew the kind of things that were said at our Gospel meetings and I also must have picked up the urgency about this message since I felt it was important to have one 'on the stocks'. It was going to be about the Lost Sheep. I was going to say that a person who didn't know Jesus was like the lost sheep and that Jesus would find them and carry them from danger to safety. What interests me about this memory is that it shows no awareness that, as my church was then constituted, I would never be in the business of preaching sermons, evangelistic or otherwise. (It's also significant that this memory pre-dates my 'conversion' experience.)

Because gender has assumed such an important place in our society, it is interesting to reflect on how I have found the church reacting to people on the basis of their gender. Although I experienced discrimination because I was a woman, I also made two interesting observations. Feminism, although it brought a new, emancipating dimension to how I thought about myself in the world, didn't finally satisfy me—it left me profoundly angry. It may become a motivating force for positive action to make life better for women, but it became dangerous for me because I turned the anger it generated on myself and blamed myself for being unable to change the sexist conditions which sometimes influenced my life. Additionally, despite what feminists said about the nefariousness of men, it was the kindness of men which was a crucial factor in my own ability to mature in this area. I do not want to present myself as a victim on this issue. Although there were difficulties, there were often choices and sometimes I didn't make the right ones. The ensuing problems were thus partly of my own strange devising.

A Brethren Girl

Although as a young child I had taken on board messages about the love of God and the urgency of salvation, I had not at that point realised that women did not preach and that therefore I would not be able to preach when I grew up. Perhaps it did not occur to me that I would not be able to use the 'sermon idea' because at that time the church had never stopped me doing anything that I wanted; the older people in it were kind and interested in me and I, in turn, enjoyed the Sunday school and the Gospel meeting—the main services I attended. It was not until my early twenties and engaged to be married that I realised how often I identified with male heroes in films and stories. As a student late one Friday night, I was watching a rather dismal B-movie, where the man went off to do daring deeds, telling his girlfriend to stay at home. All of a sudden it became clear to me that for most of my life I had been unconsciously identifying with male leads. Given that I was female, it was much more likely that I would be railroaded into a supporting part.

Although the Brethren are usually thought of as being as repressive of women, as the name implies, this is not entirely fair. 'Brethren' is the name which was given to the sect against its will. Many Brethren people would have denied belonging to any distinct grouping within the Body of Christ and only used the name when dealing with society officially, for example, when they went into hospital. Though it does show that they were perceived, like most Victorian churches, to be male-dominated, throughout their history the Brethren benefited from the ministry of a few influential female evangelists. In the 1859 revivals in Scotland Mary Hamilton and Mary Paterson were revered church planters. The Brethren also produced a significant number of female missionaries. That these women did minister shows the paramount importance of Gospel preaching among Brethren as it was through this route that many women, by becoming involved in Sunday school teaching, Gospel preaching to women or missionary service, became fully-fledged, if, publicly unacknowledged, ministers of the Word.

The mind I had been given by God enjoyed words and stories and I became good at reading, writing and talking. Because I was interested in language, I enjoyed school and found an outlet for my interests there, as well as being stimulated by a number of creative primary school teachers. During secondary school, I was beginning to be aware that if I wanted to participate in church life it was going to have to be on the church's limited terms and not on my own. Boys of my own age were commended for any stumbling, hesitant, garbled, incoherent prayers they offered in public, but I was not allowed to say a word. This was made more acute because, at school, pupils were supposed to offer answers and opinions as a matter of course, and in the Scripture Union group at school I was able to participate fully in what was happening.

Because of the advances made by the women's movement in the 1960s, during the 70s and 80s the position of women in the church became a contentious issue within the Brethren. There seemed to be quite a number of sermons about what women could or could not do, delivered with varying amounts of grace and sensitivity. I remember one preacher who found Eve guilty of several sins before she had eaten the forbidden fruit. He then argued that this categorically showed a generic weakness in women which precluded their participation in any public worship or teaching. (His argument was so watertight that it would not even allow for the teaching of women by women described in the Pastoral Epistles.) After his sermon the preacher seemed quite pleased with himself, though I was seething with indignation of behalf of myself and Eve. Part of the anger came because I could not see how to argue back—I have always found it very difficult to come up with counter-arguments and find it completely impossible to do so on the spot. The words I most wanted to hear were those of Jesus when he put a stop to the criticism of Mary of Bethany saying, 'Leave her alone.'

But they wouldn't leave us alone. They went on and on about 'submission', a sort of rhetorical bludgeoning designed to produce that very quality. Even now 'submission' has to be the word I hate most in the English language, with 'subjection' running it a close second. Its memory has the power to fill me with unspeakable fury. I hate it in summer when the sun shines and I hate it in winter when the weather is cold. I would quarantine for a decade any room in which it had been used. I would walk to the ends of the earth to exterminate the last printed example of it. If I woke up during the night I would stick pins in the eyes of it. I will never, ever believe that whatever the Bible means when it discusses 'submission' is the rank, evil, creation-denying thing preachers insisted it was.

Feminism

The fulminations of the Brethren against women seemed almost quaint by the time I got to university. The gulf between the church world and the real world was so immense that it rendered church irrelevant. And so for a couple of years it was possible to bask in the illusory pleasure that discrimination on the grounds of gender was a thing of the past. Then it became increasingly clear that, though the Brethren might be more virulent in stating their opinions on the subject of women, a great number of other men—Christians and non-Christians—held very similar views. Girls were never appointed to Christian Union presidencies—even although there was nothing apart from gender to prevent it; among the Baptists—a much more civilised group of Evangelicals whose acquaintance I had enthusiastically made—a woman could not become a Baptist minister in Scotland; and even in the Department of English at the University of St Andrews most of the lecturers were male. At this point it began to dawn on me that the problem was not just to do with frothing fundamentalists but went a good deal deeper.

I remember going into one of the libraries in University Hall in my third year of study and picking up a very elderly copy of John Stuart Mill's essay on 'The Subjection of Women' and had one of these fairly rare experiences when a bridge is constructed from the past and you are arrested by an author who seems to be speaking right into your life:

> Respecting the mental characteristics of women; their observations [those of medical practitioners and physiologists] are of no more worth than those of common men. It is a subject on which nothing final can be known, so long as those who alone can really know it, women themselves, have given but little testimony, and that little, mostly suborned.

This fitted exactly with what I had experienced in church. Women were always talked about, usually to their disadvantage, and were never allowed to speak for themselves. And here was a man—an intelligent, well-respected individual—who had cared enough to write a whole essay about it as long ago as 1869. Perhaps there was hope.

The following year I read Kate Millet's *Sexual Politics* (1977) which also made a deep impact on me because of its feminist readings. Her criticism of *Villette* (1853) stayed with me for a long time. She showed how Lucy Snow had rebelled against the inhumane ideas of women which characterised her society and then noted that it was through education—not marriage—that Lucy achieved selfhood. That section in the book resonated with me and has stayed with me ever since, but it was many years later before I could see why I had been so drawn to it.

At that point it wasn't absolutely clear to me how to integrate these arguments with my faith, but Elaine Storkey's *What's Right with Feminism?* (1985) was an excellent starter. Certain other elements of feminism I found finally frustrating. Spiritually, feminism left me feeling extremely angry. Some of the wilder assertions irritated me because of their scope and evident silliness—'All men are rapists' from Marilyn French's *The Women's Room* being a case in point, even though the novel contained many excellent insights into the way in which women were relegated to the sidelines of American society. By using a feminist analysis I could see that women were routinely treated less well than men, but unless I changed my life and relationships completely, I would not be able to get free of so much that constrained me. In fact, there would always be men to deal with. How can it possibly be right to be angry with half the human race all your life?

Attempting a *Modus Vivendi*

However, our local assembly, to which I had returned on my marriage, was a long way from being interested in which aspects of feminism I embraced and why I was less certain about others. Women could not participate in public worship. It was for real and I had better accept it. But I couldn't. Nothing in me could accept it, although I made fairly Herculean attempts to do so—sometimes for pragmatic reasons, sometimes because it seemed to me that perhaps these men were right and the Bible did say the things they said it said, sometimes because I just didn't want to be the one who seemed to want to upset the applecart. I like a quiet life. I want people to like me.

However, the desire of the Brethren to preach the Gospel meant that there was still a network of women's meetings in Ayrshire and, once I came back from university, I began to be asked to speak at these. This was the training ground where I learned how to preach. Although I didn't speak very often, I had enough engagements to work out how much could be said in twenty minutes and how to cut out everything but the main point so that at least you had said one thing clearly. I always aimed to be realistic about what I said so that I was dealing with how people really felt about things and not taking short cuts by the conventional 'sins' or 'remedies' given in standard sermons. This attempt at pastoral realism was warmly welcomed by some individuals for whom the careful distinction between what was sinful and what was not, or the naming of real sins and the demonstration of how forgiveness might work in such cases, brought a measure of relief.

Quite often on these occasions I would spend my first ten minutes or so calming down the chair person who was finding the prospect of giving out a hymn and praying at the beginning of the service quite forbidding. Though these women easily had sufficient gift for the task, they did not have the experience or the affirmation for them to feel confident about what they had to do. As usual there were notable exceptions. When invited to preach at Townhead Gospel Hall, Newmilns, either Miss Margaret Cochrane or Mrs Minnie Beggs would leave you in no doubt about what was expected of you and how you would have to stop at a particular time so that the women from Galston could catch their bus. Such confidence was delightful but rare.

I was gaining some competency in speaking and in reflecting on pastoral issues, but such gifts as I had could only be used on an intermittent basis. This outlet for humanity contrasted sharply with the Sunday by Sunday exclusion from the ordinary services of church. I suppose I could have gone off and trained for ministry in some para-church organisation or other denomination if I was so agitated about it. The fact that that didn't occur to me shows how deeply the Brethren ethos of the priesthood of the laity was engrained in me. Essentially there was no need to go elsewhere. I was a priest. The way I saw it, it was the church that was confused not me. On the one hand it was telling me I was a priest, and on the other, it was not allowing me to practise as one. The older one got, the less easy all this was to bear. So much of yourself had to be shorn off or bound up—like the feet of Chinese women—that going to church became a very destructive experience. Though quite a few male friends felt that women should have greater freedom of ministry, at that time, it was judged too divisive to do anything about it. What women were supposed to do with themselves meantime was a subject that was never openly addressed and, if you went on about it too much, you were just seen as a member of the Awkward Squad who ought to be avoided and who couldn't really be trusted. There were other more important things to be considered and it was selfish—and basically unchristian—to want more freedom for yourself.

Although I could work out that, according to 1 Corinthians 11, women had prayed and prophesied in first-century churches and I was fairly sure that the references to head-coverings were culturally specific, I couldn't make much of the references in the Pastoral Epistles banning women from teaching. This was problematic because I knew I was good at teaching and had been recruited to teach undergraduate and outreach courses at the University of Strathclyde where I was undertaking a second degree. So that left me in limbo—I thought it was likely that teaching by women was not something that God had forbidden but, with the hermeneutic I then had, I had no clear way of basing that belief on Scripture.

Anyway, all of a sudden things got a lot more complicated. During my first pregnancy there was a possibility that I was about to miscarry. I had always thought that for the first few years of my children's lives I would like to be at home with them, just as my mum had been for myself and my brothers when we were growing up. I thought, however, that I could probably do some part-time work and had accepted a post as a tutor with the Open University. The fact that the consultant couldn't say one way or another whether working would affect the rest of the pregnancy adversely or not, and the lingering idea that it might be the way God had ordered things that women ought to look after their children, coloured my thinking. I was also worried that if I worked and then miscarried, I would be blamed, or blame myself, for the death of the baby.

It was at this point that I began to co-operate in the very personally dangerous project of editing myself out of my own life. In the event I gave up the post before I had even started it—a sequence of giving up things and trying to suppress various parts of my personality in order to conform with ideas of womanhood of which I was suspicious but which I was unable to reject out of hand because I didn't have a hermeneutic which would allow me to do so. At the same time I was giving up my only formal link with education and I can see now—though I didn't then—that schools and universities had shielded me from much of the discrimination against women apparent in church life, providing me with an arena in which I could operate successfully expressing opinions and exploring issues in which I was interested. I was much more like Lucy Snow than I had realised.

The reason I couldn't see this was because I had no way of valuing—beyond commonsense and gratitude—education. The Brethren did not teach very often about creation and they didn't have a 'doctrine of creation'. When creation was discussed it was usually only to insist on a literal seven-day creation and to take pot shots at evolution. There was no consistent teaching that God was active in his creation and much of it, under human stewardship, could still be said to be 'very good'. The general idea was that the world was under judgement and the church was part of a spiritual emergency engaged in rescuing the perishing. Therefore I didn't look for God in places other than specifically religious ones because I didn't think he was interested in them. I can now see how utterly seminal educational institutions have been in God's providence in enabling me to persist in being really me and how they can be a route for many people to discover more about themselves and this world in a way that is, generally, 'very good'.

Because of that inconsistency, and because of a naturally non-confrontational personality which deeply feared rejection, I tried as hard as I could to find this contentment that everyone talked about in being at home looking after children. The rest of the pregnancy was uneventful and Katie was born safely. When I was pregnant with Mary, tests showed a higher than average chance of her being born with Down's Syndrome. Because of the risk of spontaneous abortion associated with amniocentesis, this procedure was not carried out. Although this was another false alarm, it meant that the remainder of the pregnancy was an anxious time for me.

Mary was born healthy and normal and, though I had to return to hospital for a D&C because part of the placenta was still in the womb, in all other respects the birth had gone well. However, after a life of reading and writing and studying, I did not find that looking after the house and the babies filled me with contentment. I seemed to be permanently tired. I was occasionally asked to speak either to women's groups or, on one occasion, to a workshop of men and women who were exploring issues concerning the expansion of women's role in the church. In order to prepare for this I was reading Germaine Greer's *The Female Eunuch* (1970) and I came to the section where she writes about the number of housewives on medication or some form of health supplement because they feel constantly tired:

> The housewives' life is not real: it is anachronistic and thwarting; women have been exposed to too many other kinds of life to revert to four walls and people two foot high without strain.

I could feel tears in my eyes. It was as if someone had suddenly understood exactly how I was feeling and put an arm round me. It was then I realised how much of my self-esteem was ebbing away in the round of domestic responsibilities.

I did not resent my children, or regret having them. However, the assumption often made in church was that staying at home to look after children was the best way a mother could bring up her children. For some women this is indeed the case. But it wasn't for me. I discovered I could not live with the consequences of what was, finally, my own choice. I do not agree with some of Germaine Greer's more outrageous and deliberately provocative suggestions, but that morning she got closer to the real me than anyone else had done for some time.

The Kindness of Men

However, during this time of my own project of suppressing myself, God seemed more interested in forcing me to be fully myself. My one life-line was that I had started writing for the magazine which served our churches called *Harvester* and then *Aware*. Dr Alex McIntosh, an elder at Olivet Hall, Falkirk, was involved in youth work among our churches. He had a gift for seeing how people could do things they didn't think they could do. He suggested my name to John Baigent, the book editor at *Harvester*, and I began writing book reviews which I very much enjoyed. After a short interval I was asked to become News Editor when Peter Cousins retired. I wrote snippets about what was happening in the Evangelical world and then two longer pieces of editorial material about stories in the secular news media. This brought me to the attention of a wider public and my astonishment was great when attending a Partnership Consultation at Warwick—Partnership is an organization which provides support and resources for churches in our tradition, especially when they are contemplating change. People who had only been names to me (albeit well-known names) came up and spoke to me as if they knew me and even more amazingly also took me seriously because of what I'd been writing. For once I was talking about things I was interested in other than children and the domestic round.

Some time after I began writing for *Aware*, I was asked to join the council of the fledgling Evangelical Alliance Scotland and then to represent Scotland on the EA UK Council. This brought me into contact with Evangelical writers, preachers and evangelists who had merely been names to me before. I joined the UK Council at the same time as Judith Diggins, an evangelist with the Independent Methodists, and after our first Council session, Clive Calver spoke to us saying that he had hoped that the various Evangelical 'tribes', as he called them, would begin to promote women within their own systems so that the Alliance could select women who had already come through various areas of leadership. As the 'tribes' were slow in doing this, it was up to the Alliance to keep appointing women in order to model women's roles in leadership to Evangelicals.

Whether or not this tokenism did have the normalising effect on women's ministry for which Clive hoped, it certainly improved my self-confidence. Given the deep-rooted feelings of inadequacy which I had been taught to have, the fact that when I opened my mouth in conversation, other Evangelicals who seemed to me 'famous', listened to what I said and were interested in it and engaged with me was astonishing. Although rationally I had always resisted the teaching about the role of women I had encountered, in other ways it had affected me quite deeply and it wasn't until I was physically in circumstances that contradicted it, that I could dare to believe my internal scepticism might actually be justified. I remember these council meetings in Glasgow and London as happy occasions when fellow-Christians were interested in me and what was happening in my family.

Eventually *Aware* stopped being published as it was judged to be selling too few copies. I had no obvious publication to write for and so stopped and only started writing regularly again for *Partnership Perspectives* in 2002. This is utterly in keeping with the stop-go nature of most of my public Christian life. After *Aware's* demise, Neil Summerton asked me to join the Partnership Council. I was happy to do this but again felt that I didn't know why I was there, and it took various members all their time to reassure me that I have a part to play in their proceedings.

Although this was very therapeutic for me, I still didn't seem to realise that by working I would be able to do things I enjoyed or was good at and be affirmed by that. It wasn't until my husband, Neil, took ill with chronic fatigue syndrome that it began to dawn on me that as I might need to become the sole breadwinner I had better make some realistic decisions fast. After unsuccessfully applying for jobs as a university lecturer, I trained as a teacher and began teaching English at St Aloysius College in Glasgow. As the children were getting older and I was travelling to Glasgow from Kilmarnock every day, we eventually moved to Troon where there was a half-hourly train service to Glasgow and I could walk to the station.

We began to worship at Seagate Evangelical Church which was one of the few churches in Scotland with Brethren roots which had taken the decision to widen the scope of women's ministry some years previously. This meant that, at the age of thirty-eight, I could at last participate in the weekly communion service which for me was an intensely desired, if somewhat belated, coming-of-age experience. Although Brethren were pioneers of the ministry of the laity, they did not allow women to participate in public worship when men were present. This meant that women were like children who were likewise regarded as having nothing to contribute to this occasion.

For Brethren, the Breaking of Bread was the most sacred of all their meetings. When the worshippers arrived, the communion bread and wine were on a table which could be either at the front of the hall or in the middle with the forms enclosing it on four sides. Male members of the congregation would give out a hymn or pray. The prayers centred entirely on the life and death of Jesus Christ and those which were felt to be of the greatest significance were those which were able to dwell on the mutual love of the Father and the Son. There were to be no prayers about how Christians had been blessed in salvation, nor was there to be any teaching or exhortation from Scripture, especially before the emblems had been distributed. In the church in which I was brought up, the singing at this service was unaccompanied part-singing. While there were occasions when the service seemed to drag, or when men seemed to be praying exactly the same prayer they'd prayed the week before, or when men used the occasion as a means of furthering any self-seeking agenda they might have, sometimes it produced occasions of fine Christian worship, and to be excluded from those occasions was painful.

At Seagate the elders had taken the momentous decision to allow women to participate audibly in public worship. Although their names—Neil Andrew, Ian Beckwith, Clive Conduit, Tom Hilditch, Robert McAdam, Tom

McClements, Alasdair Morrison, Graham Wallace and John Wood—may not be all that familiar to a wider Christian public, these men were persuaded by the Bible and by their consciences that this was the correct decision to take. Not that it was easy. Some Christians left the church because they felt that they could not accept that this decision did have a biblical basis. Despite the knowledge that people would leave, the decision—obviously not taken lightly given the consequences of losing members—was still taken. At that time only three other similar churches in Scotland had taken such steps and these congregations had caused some disquiet by doing so. After all the prophecies of doom which surrounded this action, the sky did not fall down. The church, with its age profile significantly younger than before, has gone on steadily and introduced a number of changes which has helped it to relate to contemporary society. For me personally, the decision has had far-reaching consequences in enabling me to worship like a Christian in church. Although the elders made the decision some years before I joined the church, I have benefited in ways I could never have guessed at before I went to Seagate and owe these men a debt of gratitude that I can never repay.

It was only when I went to Seagate that I was able to admit to myself how unhappy I had previously been. And it was all to do with one of the simplest and most profound human capacities: speech. By recognising my capacity for speech, the elders at Seagate recognised my entire humanity. I remember my first Sunday morning, standing up and praying out loud. My daughter, Mary, said that I had prayed for quite a long time and my other daughter, Katie, remarked that after thirty-eight years perhaps I had quite a lot to say. It also gave me a new view of myself as a complete human being, not one who needed to deny large parts of her personality in the presence of God.

Reflections

I no longer think that the difficulties I experienced with regard to women's role in the church were as much to do with my personal inability to accept the way things were as I was made to think. I think that any human being would find themselves reacting in such a way if they found themselves being asked to accept for themselves a life which was less than human. This is not for one moment to negate, as some feminists have done, women who find great satisfaction in the life of the home and family. There is an enduring attraction about this in which some women find their greatest joy and delight. However, not all women are the same and for those whose natures lead them in different directions, it is crucial that they should not be stymied, for it is impossible to predict how they will react when finally they can take it no longer and the kegs of resentment stored up over two or three decades finally explode the inhuman shell in which they have been living.

It is possible to live a human life within an inhuman shell. Many women I know have done this, particularly those from earlier generations. They often had fewer choices—women were not expected to work after marriage unless they had to and many women depended for financial security on their husbands. Any radical determination to lead their own lives could have led to marital breakdown, a reduced standard of living and unending pain for those around them who would have had to bear the shock of it all. Within the confines of their lives they accustomed themselves to the routine and took what they could from it, many of them developing a strong interior life through reading and through their own relationship with the Lord which helped them negotiate the restrictions they faced. And the Lord they knew was often a kinder and more encouraging figure than the rhetorical construct preachers made to stand in his place.

From all this I have observed that men vary in their attitudes to women. There are men who don't like women and men who do. Of the men who don't like women there are misogynists and chauvinists. Both groups are hostile and harmful to women especially when they're in positions of power. Some misogynists are introverted and their misogyny is often expressed in fear and avoidance. Of the men who do like women, there are those who like them because they are the same as men and those who like them because they are different. Those who like women because they are the same as men and recognise their common humanity, have characters which are often marked by justice and integrity. These men may not always feel at ease in the company of women but in the making of policy or decisions about pay scales they will not discriminate against them on the grounds of gender. Men who like women because they are different, actively enjoy the company of women because they look and sound different. This group may be chauvinist or not. The fact that it may be chauvinist is what makes a lot of human living in earlier generations of Brethren much more understandable. Although the rhetoric was extremely chauvinistic, the actual nature of relationships was substantially qualified, indeed, mollified, by the daily kindnesses they showed.

James Paton, a leader in the assembly in Beith and a preacher greatly respected by some, avowed disgust with 60s fashions and opined that 'The sisters used to be able to sit on their hair, now they can hardly sit on their skirts.' While this shows legitimate concern for the liberalisation of dress and the liberalisation of behaviour which paralleled it, it also shows that the preacher had keenly observed these changes and had ruminated on them to the extent of honing his thought into a pithy and memorable remark. This preacher also made supper for his wife every night. Both of them worked through the day—she in the house, he outside it—but in the evening, he undertook the last task of the day. The rhetoric was not always a guide to the reality. Although I have seen examples of men who are guilty of every last crime feminists accuse them of, it is at this point that I had to part company with some of the more extreme feminist statements because there is nothing more delightful than the integrity of men expressed completely through their masculinity.

However, the reason that churches need to respond more fully to women's ministry does not just have to do with the humanity of women. It has to do with the humanity of all of us. Because Brethren congregations have been built on preaching a revivalist Gospel they have not developed a mature tradition of pastoral care. Sometimes they can't even manage a bit of pastoral first aid. Women with suitable gifts incorporated into eldership would at least and at last get these issues on the agenda. Never having attended an elders' meeting, I wouldn't know, but my feeling is that pastoral care is rarely talked about unless the elders are in the middle of a full-scale scandal. I do not deny that men have pastoral gifts and are incredibly sensitive to other individuals, but generally speaking men find this area more difficult than women. There are a range of issues on which women would probably find it easier to speak to women in the first instance. Who will support the infertile couple? What will be said to the woman who has miscarried or has had a stillbirth? Would the church be able to cope with a family who had a child with a mental handicap? Or not? Or what about a family whose son or daughter finds that he or she is gay? These examples are not plucked out of the air—or from women's magazines for that matter—but from my own experience of people whose faith has been severely stunted because no one in church was able to acknowledge even the existence of these problems. I think that if the church recognises more women in leadership, it might find that it has within itself the resources to support people in Christ through life's suffering.

Women in leadership would also bring pastoral care into the eldership itself. The burdens of eldership are great. Running a church will, I guess, make Churchill's remark 'You can't please all of the people all of the time' abundantly clear and bring it home with great force. The pressure of church life is considerable and men who enter into its leadership experience it at its greatest. Sometimes it is the most gifted, the most sensitive, who buckle under the strain and in their forties and fifties withdraw from leadership altogether or experience some midlife crisis, scandalous or otherwise. Part of women's ministry might be to pastor the pastors—to identify areas of strain and to suggest strategies for dealing with it.

While I think that women could make a significant contribution to pastoral care, that's just a guess. Like J. S. Mill, I think that we don't know what will happen when women are treated like human beings. In one church they may become interested in working with old people; in another they may become whizz-kids at strategic planning—who knows? However, I do not think that men need to feel threatened by this. One of the numerous ills laid at feminism's door is that men have experienced a loss of identity since women have now proved competent at all the things men spent centuries saying their brains were too small to comprehend and their bodies were too weak to undertake. So it is important that when considering this sort of change, men—who, after all, will be the ones who implement it—see the benefits of it. Since God created men and women in his own image, if men only are in leadership only one aspect of the image is being displayed. If men and women work together in church then the full image is displayed. It is extremely important that when women are involved in leadership men do not go off in a huff or for any other reason feel excluded. Women are more likely to be interested in religion than men and if men do not maintain a highly visible role in church, other men will conclude that this is a women's thing and be put off having anything to do with it.

Women and men together are what God created and in striving to achieve it, we understand and experience more fully the joy and goodness of the redeemed creation we are in Christ. A church which displays Christian marriages, where partners love each other and stick to each other through difficulties, is going to demonstrate a message about God's love more clearly than the most eloquent preacher. A church where good, kind, decent, faithful men and good, kind, decent, faithful women participate equally in committed service of their fellow Christians and of their Lord is, without saying a word, going to make an impression on women who have been exploited and abused by men and on men who are so exasperated by women they feel they can do nothing right and that commitment is beyond them. As relationships among and between the sexes become ever more complex, a church which models the biblical pattern for such relationships is going to offer hope for men and women both.

Is it Even Possible?

Because I was working at a Roman Catholic school, just before Easter 2003 I was preparing to go on retreat with a number of senior pupils. I was discussing the programme with Damian Howard SJ, who was leading the retreat. Four talks had to be given and we talked around which titles we felt most comfortable working on. Finally Damian summed up the discussion as we ended up with the titles we felt most comfortable with. 'That's good', he said. 'You'll do two and I'll do two.' For me it was a defining moment. Here was a man who was treating me exactly the same way as he would want to be treated himself. I wasn't being asked to pray at the end as a token gesture in the direction of women's ministry or speak to a restricted audience. Indeed my gender hadn't entered into the decision at all as far as I could see. I was just a person who was being asked to help *because I could.*

CHAPTER 3

Being Sick

Being sick is extremely unpleasant. For me it usually means I wake during the night wondering why I've woken up. Then I realise I don't feel that great. Then there is the growing ghastly awareness that I am feeling waves of nausea and that I am about to vomit. The acid taste of the sickness scorches the back of my throat and is foul in my mouth. Usually my sickness is accompanied by diarrhoea which adds indignity to the other stack of miseries. Then, feeling lousy, I really must clean up the worst of it. Then back to bed with no reassurance that that will be the only bout before morning.

I have described this experience in unsparing detail because one of the main points I want to make is how horrible illness is and how that awfulness is expressed in bodily and mental pain. Illness is a disruption, an intrusion, often an indignity, a disfigurement of all the good things there can be in life. Recently I was in hospital for a routine operation on the same day as children were having teeth removed under anaesthetic. When they came round, they were in pain, their mouths were bleeding and there was no way they wanted nurses looking in their mouths to 'see how things were going on'. They just sat and howled with sore, piteous cries. Because so much pain is confined to hospitals or sick rooms and thus hidden from us, we are inclined to forget how awful illness can be; but we must never disguise from ourselves its real nature.

Being ill is a salutary reminder of the fact that we do not control our lives as much as we would like to do. Like death, illness is something that generally we do not talk about very much—often because we do not have to; we are not living under its shadow. We are incredibly fortunate living when there are excellent painkilling drugs, anaesthetics which allow life-saving surgery to take place, cures for so many illnesses which would have killed us in previous generations. The cards which we send one another say 'Get Well Soon' and for the most part we do. However, not everyone is going to get well soon. Some are not going to get well for a while, some are never going to be completely well again and others are never going to get well at all.

If we look at the world around us we see the same tension. We are intensely interested in our own health—magazines are full of diets, workouts and other advice which will keep us healthy. A great deal of this advice is useful and good. The fact that the NHS is constantly in the headlines is another aspect of our interest in health. It has become so important to us that it is one of the chief ways by which we judge our governments—how well will we be looked after when we are sick? Underlying this interest there is perhaps an unexamined assumption: we think that if we are well, we will be, in other senses, whole, by which we usually mean, happy. The corollary of this is that if we are sick we are unproductive, weak and useless.

Hospital Dramas

Our inability to control our health is seen most clearly in the number of hospital dramas which are popular viewing for large numbers of us. In these, very clear messages about health are dramatised. Your life can be changed out of all recognition in a moment. The patient could be a brickie or a Cabinet Minister but if they have both been taken into Casualty after a motorway pile-up under the swaying aid of a saline bag then they will face similar difficulties. How badly are they injured? Will they recover? Will they be able to work again? Who will support their families? Sickness often requires people to think about what is really important to them and so there are stories about deathbed reconciliations between estranged partners or family members. The plots about the deaths of children are the most difficult to watch because here we are in the territory of terrible pain of the innocents and the impossibility of saying anything about it at all. Even the kind faces of Charlie or Duffy or Carter or Abby—faces that we equate so completely with the sweetness of cure—offer no solutions.

One of the most moving storylines associated with Mark Greene from *ER* were the episodes concerned with his death from cancer. What was most interesting about them was the realism with which he faced death. In order to have his last weeks with his family, he decided to stop the chemotherapy treatment which he knew would only delay the inevitable end and would make him sick in the interim. So he spent his money—which he could not take with him—on a trip to Hawaii where he passed his final days as peacefully as possible. He enjoyed being with Elizabeth, his second wife, and their baby daughter and came to a better relationship with his tempestuous adolescent daughter from his first marriage. During this time he prepared for his own death by thinking into the future, composing letters to his daughters to be opened at various significant points in their lives. His fairly swift and early death brought a deep sadness on his colleagues who wondered why such a man who had saved so many lives should have had his life cut short.

This was an interesting return to ideas which regard death as the final event of a life during which people can sometimes assert their own values and personality. In the past Christians have talked about making 'a good death', where family and friends would sit with them as they died, in faith, and set out on the final journey. Nowadays there is sometimes a tendency to mask death with technology, as if it could circumvent the inevitable. Greene's death was the story of tragic early death, severed relationships and unfulfilled potential, but it was also the story of how a man died as he had lived, with determination, courage and love for those around him.

Thus, for all of us issues of health and illness are a source of fascination and concern. Imaginatively they dramatise for us some of the most important questions in life and lay before us a number of responses. Hospital dramas are one of the few places in modern society where all of us come near formulating or asking questions to which religion has a set of responses. We mostly avoid such questions. When we are caught up in them they shape our lives and our identities and we cannot escape their power, although we can control, to some extent, how we react to them.

Attitudes to Illness

As Evangelicals we too have been affected by the great medical advances of the last century. Many of us now have come to think of healing as some sort of spiritual 'right' which, if we cannot obtain through our doctors, we seek to obtain directly from God. And some of us do obtain it there for which we offer united and continuous thanks. However, some of us do not. Obviously if you are ill it is proper and right to pray that you may be made well again. Nobody in their right minds would want to stay ill. Health means that you are no longer so dependent on others; that you are able to be productive in ordinary life and that you stop feeling as utterly lousy as you do when you are sick. However, illness is one of the clearest and commonest signs of our broken world. Just as God has not made Christians immune to other forms of original brokenness, such as injustice, environmental catastrophe and death, so he has not made us immune to illness.

Christians who take seriously ill usually have somewhere at the back—or forefront—of their minds an expectation that God can and might heal them apart from the usual means at the disposal of doctors. This stems particularly from the ministry of Jesus which contains a number of instances of miraculous healing. This expectation may be strengthened by the beliefs of the church in which they worship as some churches confidently expect signs and wonders—in which they include healings—to accompany the spread of the Gospel. And if a person receives healing then that's fantastic and a source of great rejoicing. But what happens if you're not healed?

Given that the person was not feeling well in the first place, having hopes of healing raised then dashed is liable to lead to deflation, disappointment and even, depression. Here it is very easy to see the link between the spiritual, the mental and the physical. The unanswerable 'Why?' begins to figure in the person's thinking. Why does God heal some people and not others? Why do some people who have no time for God enjoy robust health? Why am I not healed?

The Gospel Record

One of the most pernicious answers given in such situations is that the sick person has not summoned up 'enough faith'. Poor soul. Not only are they sick, it is their own fault that they are ill. God save us and preserve us from Christians who tell us this sort of thing when we are sick. And what is this 'enough faith' anyway? According to the New Testament, God uses infinitesimal amounts of faith to achieve quite disproportionate results—if you have faith as small as a mustard seed, you can say to this mountain, 'Move from here to there and it will move' (Mt. 17.20). (Settled, hostile indifference is another matter as in Mk. 6.4-6.) Jesus never blamed anyone who came to him for being sick. The only time when he was asked about it was in the case of the blind man in John 9 when the disciples said, 'Who sinned, this man or his parents?' Jesus was quite clear that 'Neither this man nor his parents sinned...but this happened so that the work of God might be displayed in his life.' Jesus did often say that 'Your faith has made you whole', but interestingly he never said to anyone who came to him hoping for healing, 'Sorry I can't heal you—you haven't got enough faith.' And if he did not say it then, why should he have started saying it now?

The people who came to Jesus were exactly like us and came with the same sort of faith mixed with weakness that we show. One woman came thinking that if she could only 'touch the hem of his garment' she would be healed—she did not actually want to 'ask' Jesus at all for healing—she just wanted to pick his pockets for it because he was such a busy and important man she didn't want to bother him. The father with the epileptic boy was so upset about his son and so desperate for a cure that he could not tell whether he had faith or not. Those attending Jairus' daughter sent a message telling Jesus not to bother coming as there was nothing he could do. And he raised the child from the dead in an atmosphere of cynicism, unbelief and desperation. Jesus' power of healing is not constrained or magnified by our faith or lack of it.

Supposing, then, that it is not our fault that we are not miraculously healed, why, then, are Christians not commonly healed? Although we tend to think of Jesus as constantly healing, more is recorded about him as a teacher. According to John's Gospel, these healings, in addition to granting individuals relief from their suffering, were also signs which 'proved' that Jesus was the Messiah. Although both Peter and Paul performed miraculous cures, healing *per se* was not the be-all and end-all of their ministries. The first priority of both men was to extend the Kingdom by preaching the Gospel.

The attractiveness of the narratives of healing and of the compassion of Jesus which they highlight sometimes makes us think that Jesus spent most of his time healing people. A closer look at the New Testament, however, shows that the Gospel record gives much more space to his teaching and preaching. In *The Bible and Healing* (1998), John Wilkinson estimates that the number of verses devoted to healing in the Gospels varies from 9% of the total in Matthew to 20% of the total in Mark with Luke and John on 12% and 13% respectively. The number of verses devoted to oral teaching is 75% in Matthew, 50% in Mark, 66% in Luke and 64% in John. If the verses on healing are expressed as a percentage of the verses devoted to narrative—the description of events—then the percentage of verses devoted to healing rises sharply to more than a third of the total. It is still instructive to note the significantly greater amount of space given to teaching. Wilkinson goes on to point out that healings were usually illustrations of teaching rather than occasions for it and he also notes that in only *four* cases did Jesus initiate healing: the woman with the spirit of weakness (Lk. 13.12), the Bethesda paralytic (Jn. 5.6), the ear of Malchus (Lk. 22.51), and the healing of the widow's son at

Nain (Lk. 7.14). In all other recorded cases Jesus healed people who came to him or were brought to him by others. It is of course very likely that Jesus healed many more people than any of the Gospels have room to record (Jn. 21.25).

The case of the paralysed man by the pool of Bethesda is instructive. If Jesus' primary aim in ministry had been healing, then the numbers of sick people congregated in this place revered for its healing potential would have provided ample opportunity. He only healed one man. The corollary of that is that he left the rest unhealed and no specific reason is ever given for that. All that it is possible to do is look at the nature of Jesus' ministry and recognise how much of it was bound up with teaching. Wilkinson's study provides an exhaustive account of all mentions of healing in Scripture and provides comprehensive medical and biblical commentary on each. He comes to some interesting conclusions.

Even when we know God quite well, we do not like remembering that his priorities are not always ours. God's concern is not our health or wealth or happiness but our salvation which may or may not include the foregoing. God's aim in all his interactions with humankind is to bring people to this condition where he can love them and they can love him without interruption.

But this leaves God seeming uncaring and unkind—we have to suffer because it's somehow 'good' for us. God is able to help us but he is not willing for some reason of his own which he does not disclose to us. And we feel quite wrong-footed by this because 'it's not like him'—it's not at all like the God we know from Scripture and especially the Jesus we see in the Gospels. When the lepers came to Jesus for healing they seemed to be quite sure that he was able to heal them—perhaps they had heard news of Jesus which had led them to this conclusion—but they asked if he was 'willing' to heal them. And of course he was. And yet, he does not routinely heal us. We know that he will heal us eventually because in heaven there will be 'no more crying or sorrow or pain for the former things have passed away' (Rev. 21.4). So here we sit, like birds in the wilderness, with an almighty and all-loving God and a world full of things and people which need to be fixed yet are not fixed.

This tension between God's sovereignty and his love is the one most likely to derail my faith altogether, and only the continual bolstering of Scripture, and the witness of Christian friends who cope better with the tension, keep my faith from coming off the tracks. It is not the abstract formulation of the problem which bothers me so much as the grief which I observe in the lives of those around me. And if I am absolutely honest with myself, somewhere under all the polite rationalisings and all the proper justifications of God's character, some part of me blames that grief on God. He could stop it and he does not, so it is his fault. I like to think that the part of me that blames God is small; but when I reach those aspects of my personality, they are vast tracts of boiling volcanic rage which actually frighten me because of their size and uncontrolled fury. Yet I turn up, meek and mild, Sunday by Sunday, in church and to look at me you would not think I would say boo to a goose.

There are ways of dealing with these issues but at the moment I want to leave the tension raging at its height with all its power to disturb in order to show the psychological pressures to which seriously ill Christians may be subject in addition to the debilitating effects of their illness. It is more likely that they will blame themselves for not having 'enough faith' to get better, but it is possible that resentment of God's ways may also be present. It is also possible that the former is used to suppress the latter. Not all Christians may react in this way, not all may be aware of these forces or aware of them to this degree, and certainly most would find it difficult to admit to them. I do not like admitting to it myself—it makes me feel ashamed that I cannot always hold on to the great signals set out in Scripture which will guide me safely home and yet I get intensely fed up with living as if these reactions did not exist, as if, if we confessed our deepest worries to God, he would have to go and lie down in a darkened room because he could not cope. The depths of our inability to believe even when in so many other ways we do believe and we want to believe may be news to us; it is not to God. Jesus knows the dimensions of our unbelief intimately and comprehensively because 'he bore our sins in his own body on the tree'.

So let's leave difficult reactions to sovereignty for a moment and look at the other side of the tension: the awareness that God loves us and cares for us, particularly when we're ill. This is seen clearly in Luke's Gospel where he catalogues the symptoms of illness and their effects on people's lives. He describes 'a woman...who had been subject to bleeding for twelve years, but no one could heal her.' Many manuscripts record that she had spent all that she had on doctors (Lk. 8.43). Luke notices how long she had been sick and the financial implications. That in itself means that she had had to change her priorities and spend her money on health care when perhaps she had had other plans. Who knows what precious ambitions had been destroyed by this illness? Luke also describes the plight of the man possessed by the demon, Legion, living among tombs and cutting himself with stones—a picture of dereliction and neglect (Lk. 8.30). Matthew lists the people who came to Jesus: 'those suffering severe pain, the demon-possessed, those suffering seizures, and the paralyzed'. And then he records simply 'and he healed them' (Mt. 3.24).

When Jesus is dealing with sick people he is very kind to them. He takes Jairus' daughter by the hand and, when she wakes, tells her parents to give her something to eat. He asks Blind Bartimaeus, 'What do you want me to do for you?', not barging in with divine healing but listening for the man's assessment of what he wants Jesus to do. He makes the woman, who had been crippled by a spirit for eighteen years, straight, and in doing so brings her out of the twilight zone she had inhabited. She had spent eighteen years looking at the ground, seeing people's feet and the borders of their clothes. Before he healed her, he called her forward and for a time this stooped creature, whom people felt it best to ignore, was the centre of attention (Lk. 13.10-17). Jesus was not afraid of illness and his healings produced not only spiritual and physical healing but social integration as well.

There are many places in Scripture where it is obvious that God understands the devastation that illness causes and in Jesus there is a depth of care for the whole sick person which is exceptional. So how does this apply to the sick person today? The alternative to instant and permanent healing is living with illness and it is my conviction that this is the Christian reality to which many of us are called.

A Personal View

My husband in his twenties and thirties when I knew him first was an extremely active person. He played squash and badminton and was a keen hill-walker. Hillwalking is a euphemistic expression which actually means climbing small mountains. In Scotland 'hills' over 3,000 feet are called Munros and some hillwalkers—'Munro-baggers'—aim to climb all of them and organise a day's walking so that they will be able to 'bag' several peaks in the one day. In addition to his hill-walking, he was also active in our church and ran the youth work and regularly spent his Sundays preaching. He also decided that he would like to begin a part-time PhD on the history of Christian Brethren churches in Scotland—the movement we both belonged to. Towards the end of the summer of 1992 he took one of the viral infections he had taken regularly during our marriage. This one seemed to be dragging on for a long time without any obvious improvement. Neil visited the doctor who did some tests. The next day the doctor arrived at the door—a thing unheard of. He explained that the virus was severe and that Neil should stay in bed and not try to do anything strenuous.

However, Neil simply did not regain his strength. The GP said that Neil was the first patient he had personally observed whose viral condition developed into post-viral fatigue, sometimes called chronic fatigue syndrome, or ME, or yuppie flu. In this first period he was off work for six months—then he got back to work—then the symptoms re-appeared and he was off his work for fourteen months. He felt continuously tired. He also had headaches and sore fluish feelings in his limbs. In the acute phase he just ate and slept.

This made him intensely frustrated because there were so many things he wanted to do and he could not get on with them; his ability to plan for the future was completely destroyed.

As the months passed all these things which had been so important moved to the margins of his life and his single aim was to get back to work. I was looking after our two daughters at this stage and was not in employment so it was crucial that Neil return to work if we were to be able to live as we had been doing. The school was helpful and enabled Neil to make a graduated return to teaching (a fairly active job in which it is not possible to 'pace' your work). He did manage this in a struggle which seemed to me heroic. He came home at 3.30 and went to bed until it was time to have our evening meal. At weekends he was often exhausted and spent most Saturday mornings in bed.

This chronic illness had various effects. He was not able to do half the things he had done before and even things most people take for granted, such as going out for a coffee on a Saturday afternoon or going on a short break, were not possible—he would just be too tired and have to sleep. It changed what was possible for him as an individual and for us as a family. His ambitions had to change. Since then he has persevered with his academic study—most of it can be done from home with occasional library trips. It is sedentary and therefore does not require a great deal of physical energy. *Brethren in Scotland 1838-2000* was published in 2003.

In February 2001 our elder daughter Katie began to suffer from headaches. After a fairly prolonged period of medical investigation, the doctors, having eliminated some of the scarier things, decided that she, too, was suffering from chronic fatigue syndrome. Even as the consultant was uttering the phrase 'chronic fatigue syndrome' I remember in a panicky sort of way thinking that I ought to be pushing the words back into his mouth. So deeply did I not want to hear that diagnosis, I had not even entertained it as a possibility during the investigations. At the moment Katie attends school part-time after having been ill for over four years.

While many Christians have prayed about both these situations, in both of them it has been our experience that healing has come about much in the way that it is usual to experience it in these illnesses. It took about two years for Neil to weather the worst of it and get back to work, but during the intervening years his fitness has varied, improvements and relapses punctuating a pattern of slow improvement. Given that there was no instantaneous permanent cure for either of them, our experience of God has been of one who helps you live with illness.

Support During Illness

Various factors have helped in this. The first is the Welfare State. We were very fortunate that the first GP Neil saw was able to diagnose and care for him during his illness. It is difficult to explain just what a source of strength and comfort a good GP is in what was for us a very frightening situation, and we praise God that in our country high quality medical care is freely available to all who need it. In addition we were able to benefit from sick pay which kept the family going through the crisis of Neil's absence from work. This, too, meant that we were shielded from the most serious consequences of illness. We were very aware that the level of social provision in Britain was one of the chief means through which God provided for us practically during our difficulties and very grateful for the Socialists, Trade Unionists and Christians who campaigned for these universal benefits.

Apart from this, Neil also saw a homeopathic doctor who is quite used to seeing the cases the NHS cannot cure. In addition to any medicines she prescribed, she had longer appointments and was able to listen to how Neil's condition was manifesting itself and give good advice on how he should try to manage his condition. This became even more important after the GP who looked after Neil initially moved away. Not all GPs are as clear in their own minds that chronic fatigue syndrome has an objective reality and, if a good doctor is a blessing, a doctor who thinks a patient is not ill when the patient is telling him he is, just makes the situation worse, usually by instilling doubt in the patient's mind. In turn this can lead to the patient making physical effort to overcome his or her 'non-existent' illness which leads to a relapse and to a less buoyant mental world where the patient feels it is no use telling the doctor anything because they are not believed by the doctor.

In terms of Katie's health, the NHS consultant provided a range of therapists: a medical consultant, a physiotherapist, a psychologist, and a point of contact for all the agencies involved in Katie's care including the school. The link between all these services was of significance. It allowed the school to see Katie's case from the point of view of doctors and parents and was the impetus for their crucial action in supporting the request for home tuition. We were very grateful for all this help, although it has to be said taking your child for a series of appointments with highly qualified people who cannot cure her does become dispiriting. However, it does show a level of concern which goes beyond the merely technical—the 'if-we-can't-cure-you-we-don't-want-to-know-you-attitude'. As a family we did feel well-looked after and are glad that we were not neglected by the medical profession. Initially, at least. Later, as long as you're not seriously ill, you're often left to get on with it.

The second source of strength was our extended family. Both Neil's parents and my own, who lived in the same town as us, became much more involved in childcare than they might otherwise have been. Other family members kept in touch and often provided practical help of many kinds. Friends, too, were very important especially in terms of personal well-being. Sometimes it is easier to discuss feelings and frustrations with friends, and also where you see things going in the longer term. During the illness we had a few extremely significant friends—Christian and non-Christian alike—who supported us and made things more bearable. We realised that if one family member is sick, then that affects the whole family and redistributes tasks which might otherwise be shared. As the 'well' partner I sometimes got fed up doing things on my own and, because I like being organised, I found the inability to plan even such simple things as who was going out to Sunday services, when the children were young, frustrating.

There were some attitudes which did make life more difficult, especially, I think for Neil. These were almost all tied up with Christianity. He was a well-respected preacher and teacher and spoke quite regularly at a variety of services. He had also written for the magazine of our group of churches and his intelligence and spiritual insight were much appreciated. When he became ill, this source of approbation dried up and there was not much to replace it. Evangelicals are activists and when someone ceases to be active his brothers stretcher him off and leave him lying at the side of the pitch where he is tormented by the cries coming from the excitement of the match still in progress. It is as if an entire Christian life has been thrown away.

A Range of Attitudes

Some people, who might have come to see how things were going, never got round to it. Some people were too busy. But people usually do what they want. What is it that prevents people visiting the sick? Some people simply think of visiting sick brothers and sisters as less important than preaching and teaching. I have also come to believe that some people actually hate and fear illness presumably because of the disruption it brings and the curtailment of common ambitions it forces on people. Thus, when someone is sick, they feel, probably quite rightly, that they have nothing in common with the sick and would have nothing to say to them if they visited them. While this may be the case, it's worse than useless for the sick person because he feels quarantined, a source of contamination. I think there are very deep fears about illness which all our medical knowledge and knowledge about the workings of hospitals have done little to expel. The chief of these is that the sick contaminate the well.

Another difficulty was that some people just would not accept that the condition showed no betterment. Some people are so remorselessly optimistic that they can interpret any catalogue of symptoms as improvement. This sometimes happened when people asked for Neil. I often went about with a little 'bulletin' in my head which I changed weekly and duly gave out to anyone who asked for him. I used to envy royalty because all they had to do was post their bulletin on the gates of Buckingham Palace. There was one man who assiduously asked for Neil and would listen to the unchanging list of symptoms and then say, 'So he's feeling a little better this week?'

Another attitude was that prayer would heal. Praying with Christian friends almost invariably brought relief in terms of the solidarity of the church with you during suffering, and the willingness of God to bless and take care of you in such situations. But this idea, that if we prayed God would do some miracle, rankled. In the first place, it made ordinary Christians, who were fairly sure that God was not going to heal miraculously, not come to pray because they felt there was no point in praying. This cut us off from one of the most health-giving activities available to Christians. Not only did we not get a miracle, we did not get the general benefit that comes from opening ourselves up to God with our brothers and sisters. Secondly, we sometimes got the impression from some people that we were not really serious about God or about getting better because we had not pursued this route. This made me apoplectic with rage which I rarely expressed to the person who seemed so solicitous about our welfare—we didn't get so many notes of interest that we could afford to be choosy about them. So we said thank you very much, how interesting, yes, we'll think about it, we'll be in touch. But honestly, who did these people think they were talking to? We were facing a situation we had never wished for, it was difficult in living one day at a time and frightful in terms of the future possibilities—at one stage I thought Neil was never going to get any better ever—obviously if miracles could be had for the pleading we would have obtained one.

Some Reflections

At that stage I came to the conclusion that miracles were mysterious things. I was fully persuaded that God sometimes worked such things but I wasn't even happy about saying that in our case he didn't want to. I think God loved us very much during that unhappy time. Given how much our own earthly mothers and fathers did for us, I cannot conceive that God felt any less than they did. If you say he can perform miracles but he won't he's made out to be uncaring. If you say he wants to but he doesn't he sounds indifferent. If you say he wants to but he can't he sounds weak. But we know that God is neither uncaring nor weak, therefore none of the above statements can be fully true. That's why I invoke the category of mystery.

Having said that, perhaps that is to invoke the mysterious too quickly. There are some other aspects of God's behaviour that we should consider. The first is: is there a difference between the miraculous and the non-miraculous, the natural and the supernatural? Why do we think it is 'natural' that the sun rises every day? Why do we think it is 'natural' that seeds grow into wheat which when milled into flour can be baked into bread? Why is it 'natural' that parents love their children? These are the foundational processes on which our lives are based but they are processes which were created by God. They are marvellous and life-giving processes but we are so used to them we take them for granted. Sometimes it is easier to view all God's actions as 'supernatural' because everything that he created out of nothing is permeated by splendour and wonder when you give it more than two seconds consideration. Yet, this broken creation is to be redeemed by suffering, not by miracle. It is therefore likely that the redeemed will triumph, as the Saviour did, by suffering and not by miracle. The Resurrection, the creative power of God blasting a way through the strata of stone that is death into the new sort of life on the other side, vindicated the work of redemption which was completed in its entirety on the cross. Our expectation should be suffering, not miracle. Luke's understanding is of suffering and then glory as Jesus, the vindicated Messiah, makes clear in his teaching to the two on the road to Emmaus. John's understanding is even more profound because he sees the glory as the suffering. In the Upper Room discourses Jesus says that he will be glorified *in his crucifixion.*

This is an idea which unsettles us because it is so 'unnatural'. As Christians we want to keep the categories of glory and suffering miles apart. Yet John, who reflects so profoundly on the ministry of Jesus, comes up with this searching conclusion that the glory is the suffering. This is hard for us because, in our culture, there is a great deal of thought, expressed constantly through advertising, which leads us to formulate the greatest good as a pain-free life of pleasure. There is no place for suffering and the idea that suffering could bring its own blessings is intermittent (though it did arise in the *ER* plot about Mark Greene). Now while Christianity does not teach that you should go looking for suffering, and it is right that you should stay out of its way when you can, it also reckons that for most people suffering is unavoidable. Moreover, the idea that suffering may bring its own blessings is firmly rooted in the death of Christ of whom the prophet said:

> After the suffering of his soul, he will see the light of life and be satisfied. (Is.53.11)

God does meet with his suffering people in their pain and distress.

However, there are issues here to be avoided. God does not make people suffer in order to 'teach them lessons'. It is rather that, even during suffering when it comes, he can develop us through it. We are also free during suffering to reject God's voice. Suffering does not always produce sweetness and patience—it can quite often produce bitterness and anger. If we find someone reacting to suffering in this way we cannot sit in judgement on them and say they ought to accept what is happening to them. We have no idea how we would react if we were in their shoes. We must help and carry their burdens as best we can. Perhaps if we wait patiently with them, they will come to see things differently.

Secondly we cannot tell people glibly that suffering is good for them or even that it is God's will. The only approach with those in distress is to sit with them and continue to sit with them until things change. Of all the Christian virtues, faithfulness is the one that counts most with the distressed. You don't need to say anything which is great because, actually, there isn't anything to say. You don't need to bring anything. You don't need a profound understanding of Scripture. You just need to be there. When Christ was at the height of his suffering on the cross asking why God had forsaken him, why this suffering had landed on him, no-one piped up with the idea that this was God's will (which it was) or that this suffering would be good for him (which was also true) or that 'all things work together for good' (which was true). Although the vastness of the agony doesn't invalidate any of these truths, it does make their expression at that point inappropriate. Evil has its numinous penumbra which precludes idle chatter. Sometimes in the presence of suffering brothers and sisters, fellow-Christians, would do well to keep their mouths shut.

Because Evangelical churches cannot readily conceive of any other ways of serving Christ than active ones, they are not always great places for sick people to be. Sick people are no longer able to be involved in the same way that they used to and this exclusion adds to the misery of the illness. Yet, it is my conviction that Christians who bear the suffering of illness are not marginal to the purposes of God, but central. They look to the world (and often to fellow-Evangelicals) as Jesus did when he was on the cross—failures, defeated, rejected, despised and as those 'from whom men hide their faces' (Is. 53.3). Yet they bear this suffering in the context of their faith. Perhaps they bear it in great weakness of faith, or, in moments of infuriated wrestling with the mysterious purposes of God, yet, despite everything, they find themselves still believing in the revelation of God in Jesus Christ. Do they not, as Paul suggests, 'fill up in [their] flesh what is still lacking in regard to Christ's afflictions, for the sake of his body, which is the church (Col. 1.24)? When Job's life had collapsed around him and he was scraping his sores with a bit of broken pottery, his wife told him to 'Curse God and die' (Job 2.9). She recognized that though nothing could be done about the situation, a person could take comfort in venting his spleen against the God who allowed such misery. Although Job is eloquent about the injustice of his plight, he also recognizes the justice of God even though what he is most aware of is the pain of the gap between the two positions which is demonstrated in his bodily agony. Could this anguished believing be an opaque pane through which we discern, muddily, the fact that there is significance in a person's suffering, that there is something in it which on the one hand expresses the drama of the sinner who can do nothing to attain salvation, and, on the other, expresses the love of the Saviour, who, at immense personal cost, drinks the cup the Father gives him? Isn't it this suffering-in-faith through which Christians in supreme weakness take up their crosses and follow Christ? And might not stumbling along the Via Dolorosa after Jesus be just as important an exhibition of the grace that there is in the Gospel as there is in an outstanding evangelistic address?

Sick Christians should not be shunned in their suffering but cared for: partly because this is the compassionate response enjoined on Christians, but partly, also, because of the close bond of suffering they share with Jesus himself.

How Should Churches Treat the Sick?

When Jesus met sick people he was always kind to them. Even though we can't effect a cure, kindness should not be beyond any of us. Someone with pastoral sensitivity should head up this ministry. That person should be seen as the interface between the sick person and the church. They should aim to find out whether the person wants details of their condition to be known; whether they want their name to be mentioned in public prayer; whether they want visitors; whether they need practical help—like getting to hospital or having children looked after to allow hospital visits to be made or needing meals or shopping done when they come out. Along with this person, there should be a number of people who are willing to visit the sick. These people need to be willing, be able to pray simply and briefly, be able to listen to what the sick person is saying and to be able to keep their visits short. They should also be able to report any improvement or deterioration to the person in charge.

The church should see the visitation of the sick as an important part of its ministry and should encourage and equip all members to pay calls on sick people as a matter of course; it is what Christians *do*, just as praying or worshipping or giving to charity is what Christians do.

Some people are more than averagely gifted in this area. In any congregation it is important to find out who these people are and see whether there is anything that can be done to enable them to minister in this way. These people should also be acknowledged and valued. Although looking after those who are ill sometimes involves issues of confidentiality and may therefore have to be done out of the public eye, at some time every year in the calendar of the church these people ought to be recognized and thanked, and every few years perhaps a dinner might be given in their honour as the church makes clear the priority it puts on sick people and their care. As Christians we are far too good at taking the service of others for granted. Sometimes the first time they'll hear 'Well done' will be when Christ says it to them in glory. Gratitude is a Christian virtue and we ought to display it to each other now because it is a tremendous means of maintaining motivation. Just because people are doing it 'to the Lord' doesn't mean their service is automatic. It costs effort and determination and perseverance and those are qualities we must revere.

Obviously this is a counsel of perfection and not all congregations will have the personnel or energy to put it into practice. However it remains true that the easiest way of measuring the reality of pastoral care in a congregation is by looking at how it looks after its weakest (sickest) members.

Sick people may be important spiritual teachers. The Apostle Paul, whom we normally regard as a maker of great journeys and founder of churches, suffered intermittently from what he called a 'thorn in the flesh'. Many of the possibilities of what this illness was are outlined in John Wilkinson's *The Bible and Healing*. The author notes that Paul was used to heal others and that he recognized gifts of healing as gifts of the Holy Spirit. And when he himself fell ill he immediately prayed that he would be made well. Instead God told him that this burden was necessary to prevent him from becoming excessively spiritually proud. Paul lived out the life of Christ in sickness and in health, imprinting on uncontrollable experience his own values. Paul received no instant, permanent cure. Not for him the cool touch of the healing fingers of Jesus. Instead, the tremendous comfort he received in the promise, 'My grace is sufficient for you; my strength is made perfect in weakness' has been multiplied to suffering Christians living with illness throughout subsequent centuries (2 Cor. 12.9).

A prayer about illness:

I will trust him whatever, wherever I am. I can never be thrown away. If I am in sickness, my sickness may serve him; in perplexity, my perplexity may serve him; if in sorrow, my sorrow may serve him. He does nothing in vain.

J. H. Newman (1801-90).

CHAPTER 4

The Jesus We Want and the Jesus We've Got

My own experiences in the church and the circumstances of Neil and Katie's illnesses led me to re-examine the life of Jesus in the Gospels. I had had a simple rather than a dramatic conversion. I had been excluded from the public ministry of the church—or only engaged in it on women-only terms—and the experience of chronic illness in the family had led to a functional separation from many of the healthy members of the church. Meanwhile, the church carried on as if none of these difficulties existed. The impression I was left with was that if I was experiencing difficulties it was my fault; there was something wrong with me. In addition the church also talked about the omnipotence of God and the possibility of revival, but we rarely saw acts of stupendous might and only very few conversions. These were just more of the ideas that we all lived by but which I, secretly, felt did not work. Perhaps they worked for other people, although I had my doubts. This all seemed more than a bit pointless when we were supposed to be spreading the Good News of the Kingdom. How could we tell people that God could be with them in their difficulties if we did not feel that he had been with us in ours?

It seemed to me that God worked in quiet, unobtrusive ways which could, indeed, have great impact but I was convinced that he did not have a magic wand although this was what our assumptions implied. The implication that we wanted him to do magic did seem far away from the piety and sincerity of the Christians among whom I lived. Still there was some sort of mismatch. The trouble for me was that in my early years I had also subscribed to this notion that Jesus was a figure in some ways not unlike Superman—he had supernatural powers which allowed him to overcome difficulties instantly and stories such as the stilling of the storm or the feeding of the 5,000 seemed to support this sort of idea.

However, it was becoming a wearisome business living within an Evangelicalism which was not interested in raising, never mind answering, these questions as a matter of course. Evangelicalism sometimes presents itself like a big Sunday school. Everything is happy and bright and simple. While there are advantages in this for children, it becomes stultifying for intelligent or suffering adults whose minds or experiences mean that they come up with questions about how their faith relates to what happens in church. Instead of being seen as the outcome of the activity of the Holy Spirit in their lives, these questions are often seen as unnecessarily troubling and are easily to be set aside as Evangelicalism trundles merrily on with its 'one size fits all' rhetoric of sanctification. There was a gap between the truth the church proclaimed and the reality some Christians faced.

The Gospels always seemed to be the place where this illness-free, miracle-working, purposeful life was possible and where there was no gap between appearance and reality. Apart from the Lord, there was no one I knew during that time that I could discuss these thoughts and accompanying feelings with on a regular basis. So I laid them before the Lord and began reading through the Gospels along with N. T. Wright's *Jesus and the Victory of God* (1996). This is an academic book—a contribution to studies on the historical Jesus. I have not mastered the book's erudite contents and have only read it as a layperson with no academic background in this area. So what follows are the sorts of things that occurred to me after having read Wright, and who knows whether I have read Wright correctly? It is just what happens when an ordinary Christian tries to understand her faith a bit better by extending her reading. The transfiguration, for example, started to become important for me, but this is not an incident which figures largely in books on the historical Jesus because of the way in which the academic discourse is constructed. What follows, therefore, is not an academic essay but a devotional reading of Scripture, influenced by Wright.

The Identity of Jesus

The Gospels' hottest topic is the identity of Jesus of Nazareth. He is seen healing people, carrying out exorcisms, performing miracles, talking, teaching, debating and telling stories. People, amazed at the things he does, ask, 'Who is this?' (Mt. 21.10). Sometimes these questions have an edge of irritation about them as Jesus claims to have special power. 'Who is this who even forgives sins?', say onlookers when Jesus forgives the 'kind of woman' whose love Jesus accepted but whose presence shocked Simon the Pharisee. (Lk. 7.49). Sometimes it is Jesus' power over the elements which provokes this question, 'Who is this? He commands even the winds and the water, and they obey him?' (Lk. 8.25)

The answer to this question was vital for believing people. If God was speaking through a prophet, or, if indeed, he had sent the Messiah, then it was essential to follow Jesus. If Jesus was simply another healer-exorcist-radical leader then you might follow him or not but the decision was of a different order. Jesus himself, interested in these reactions, asked his disciples who he was taken to be and received this answer:

> Some say John the Baptist; others say Elijah; and still others, that one of the prophets of long ago has come back to life. (Lk. 9.19)

In the days before constant news bulletins, Jesus and John were similar enough to cause confusion. Those who thought Jesus was Elijah might have been thinking about the prophecy in Malachi, 'See I will send you the prophet Elijah before that great and dreadful day of the Lord comes' (Mal. 4.5). Elijah was revered as the greatest of the prophets and the fact that people were willing to make this identification shows how much they respected Jesus and pushed his identity towards that of the Messiah. However, in John's Gospel Jesus explains that John the Baptist is the second

Elijah preparing the way for the Messiah. Both of these identities—John or Elijah—are hedging round the underlying issue of the closeness of those identities to that of the Messiah. When Jesus asks his disciples who they think he is, Peter, profoundly, if momentarily, inspired, declares that Jesus himself is the Messiah.

So you would think that that would be it, wouldn't you? Bingo. Twelve assorted fishermen and hangers on have hit the religious jackpot. The Messiah, long-promised, whom every devoted Jew since Genesis 3.16 had expired desiring to see, had arrived, and they were his chosen companions. Jesus of Nazareth is the Messiah. The Day of the Lord has come. We are his special friends. O joy. O delight. Yet at that very point the scene goes dark. Jesus—instead of dwelling on the implications his disciples seem to have associated with this declaration—begins to talk to them about his view of his final destiny which encompasses ignominy and defeat at the hands of the Jerusalem establishment.

Peter begins to remonstrate with Jesus, 'Never, Lord', he says. 'This shall never happen to you!' This response, which shows Peter wanting to shield Jesus from suffering, provokes one of the sharpest responses Jesus ever uttered to anyone who followed him:

> 'Get behind me, Satan! You are a stumbling block to me; you do not have in mind the things of God, but the things of men'. (Mt. 16.23)

Because Peter's response had no room for suffering, it had no real conception of the scale of the problem Jesus faced and the means at his disposal to resolve it.

Jesus was faced with a nation which smouldered with resentment against its Roman occupiers. Many of them were looking for a leader who would lead them against the Romans as the Maccabees had fought against the pagan rule of Antiochus Epiphanes. He was faced with a religious establishment which had squeezed grace out of religion and replaced it with law. Their regulations were so numerous and fierce that it was difficult for poor people to keep them and they were regarded as second-class citizens. Some could not get close to the Temple in Jerusalem—such as those who were sick, those who were demon-possessed, and those who were not respectable.

Jesus chose not to become a nationalistic leader. He advocated paying taxes to Caesar and giving to God what belonged to him. He included the Roman occupier in his ministry when commending the simple faith of the centurion (Lk. 7.9). He included the Samaritans in his ministry, advocating peaceful relations with them even when they did not invite him into their villages. This was in contrast to his disciples who wondered if Jesus would like them to 'call fire down from heaven to destroy them?' (Lk. 9.54) Although Jesus preached mainly to Jews, mere nationality was not a basis for exclusion. Jesus clearly saw the implications for Israel if it rose up against the Romans:

> O Jerusalem, Jerusalem, you who kill the prophets and stone those sent to you, how often I have longed to gather your children together, as a hen gathers her chicks under her wings, but you were not willing. Look your house is left to you desolate. (Lk. 13.34)

Jesus also clearly saw that his heart's desire to 'establish his Kingdom'—a way of living which existed in people's hearts and minds and therefore transformed social structures—would bring him into head-on collision with the Jewish authorities, especially as his followers were often drawn from those groups marginalised by religious professionals. But, just as he did not see the Romans, though cruel, as the real enemy, so he did not see the religious authorities, though inadequate, as the real enemy. In and behind those institutions Jesus discerned the forces of evil and he knew that they could not be overcome by political or ecclesiastical means. Neither a new kingdom (politically defined) nor a new church (whatever the future might hold) was the answer. Only God could win such a battle. The conflict between himself and the authorities which Jesus foresaw was to be the crucible in which the forces of evil could be engaged in all their ferocity and finally be overcome.

So when Jesus calls Peter 'Satan', he is not kidding. After the temptations in the wilderness, the devil left him until 'an opportune time' (Lk. 4.13). It must have been disconcerting to hear him speaking through Peter, one of his closest friends, and one who had moments before by the help of 'my Father in heaven' recognised Jesus as the Messiah. Messiah, yes. But what kind of Messiah? If Jesus could not even enable Peter and the others to accept a suffering Messiah, how was he going to get the idea over to anyone else? If Peter was completely bamboozled by this idea and John, the very individual sent to prepare the way for him, sent his own disciples over to ask if Jesus was the Messiah, then it was going to be exceptionally difficult to get the message over at all.

What Sort of Messiah?

This is indicated in the strange warning to the disciples not to tell anyone that he was the Messiah. Jesus knew that he would have to spend time training the disciples to accept this vision. John had shown the way with the message that people should be baptised to show that they turned away from their sins. Jesus built on that and, like John, appealed to the common people. John enabled them to receive forgiveness wherever they were ready to receive it, thus bypassing the Temple system and making those whose livelihoods depended on that system very angry. Given how radical Jesus was, it is not surprising that he was crucified, only that he survived as long as he did. (In John's Gospel, Jesus is shown to be very sensitive on this issue. Indeed, his understanding of what he calls his 'time' is a significant element of his own spirituality. He has a strong sense of when God is giving him time to teach and when God calls him to suffer. Quite often he will say, 'My time has not yet come' contrasting with his prayer in the Upper Room as he anticipates Calvary, 'Father, the time has come.')

Nor was it simply his enemies Jesus had to circumvent. In the aftermath of the feeding of the 5,000, his supporters proved problematic. This miracle is usually placed after

Jesus hears the news of John's death. In John's death the forces of evil were cruelly apparent and so were the consequences of making political statements. John had condemned Herod for marrying his brother Philip's wife. Finally after Herod had arrested John, Philip's wife manipulated Herod into executing John. John, the last and greatest of the prophets, died for speaking out righteously against an unrighteous regime. Jesus could expect no different treatment.

Yet with all these problems about revealing his identity, training his disciples to understand that the Messiah had to suffer, avoiding confrontation until the time was right, the next episode recorded in the Gospels (the reaction of Jesus to the death of John?) is the feeding of the 5,000. This miracle is beautiful in its scope, and calm. First of all, it feeds hungry people. Secondly, it would bring to Jewish minds the earlier miracle of God supplying manna for his people in the desert. It would also recall the feeding of 100 people by Elisha in 2 Kings 4.42. Messiah or not, for some in the crowd it was just too good to be true and they decided that life under Jesus would be much better than life under any other earthly ruler they had come across and so 'they intended to come and make him king by force' (Jn. 6.15). Again Jesus comes close to political events because of the actions of his supporters but he chooses not to engage and evades them, withdrawing into a mountain place by himself.

Jesus was constantly challenged to enter the arena of earthly power in order to establish his kingdom. Perhaps it was his chief temptation, the one Satan put his finger on when he said:

> I will give you all their authority and splendour for it has been given to me, and I can give it to anyone I want to. So if you worship me it will all be yours. (Lk. 4.6-7)

There it is again. The easy glory. A life where suffering is not even mentioned. And that is the point. There are no such human lives. Suffering and sin disfigure everything. What Satan promises is illusory. 'Authority and splendour' are not his to give; he is lying. His sort of 'authority and splendour' are shot through with every sort of corruption and are utterly transient. Jesus declares that he will only ever worship God, thus foreclosing any further discussion on aims.

A Suffering Messiah

What about the means Jesus will use to achieve his aims? Given that the enemy is Satan and the evil powers that he controls and the consequences of his influence on earth are lives blighted by suffering, how will Jesus defeat the foe? Jesus' vision is the way of suffering. He hands himself entirely over to God. Then, as, under God, the forces of evil are unleashed against him, God accepts his sacrifice and the power of Evil is defeated. Jesus says: 'But I, when I am lifted up from the earth, will draw all men to myself' (Jn. 12.32); and 'unless an ear of wheat falls to the ground and dies, it remains only a single seed. But if it dies, it produces many seeds' (Jn. 12.24); and 'For the Son of Man did not come to be served but to give his life a ransom for many' (Mk. 10.45).

In each of these sayings Jesus sees his death as the means by which his aim will be achieved. He tells Pilate that in the final conflict they will not need swords. 'My kingdom is not of this world. If it were, my servants would fight to prevent my arrest by the Jews.' Although when referring to the coming crisis, Jesus advises the buying of a sword, he seems more to be indicating the extent of the crisis than advocating the use of violence, even in self-defence. As soon as he finished speaking, the disciples produce two swords and Jesus is lukewarm about their existence (Lk. 22.36-38). Right to the end he refuses to use force. Peter, who has still not fully understood the kind of project Jesus is involved in, has a sword and uses it to cut off the ear of the servant of the High Priest. Jesus says 'Put your sword away! Shall I not drink the cup the Father has given me?' (Jn. 18.11). Jesus also comments on the cowardice of the authorities because of the way they come armed to the teeth to arrest him and he also stresses who his real opponent is:

'Am I leading a rebellion, that you have come with swords and clubs? Every day I was with you in the temple courts, and you did not lay a hand on me. But this is your hour—when darkness reigns.' (Lk. 22.52-3)

It is clear from this that Jesus did not see earthly power as his sole objective and in trying to establish his 'Kingdom' he refused to use overtly political means, either peaceful or violent, to achieve his ends. For Jesus, the political route was a snare, not because there is anything wrong with politics *per se*, but because political means were not large enough in scope for the ends he had in view. He needed something altogether larger and more profound.

Glory

So where does the glory fit in? Glory is part of God's character. Where do we see glory in the story of Jesus? In the Gospels the transfiguration is situated after Peter's confession that Jesus is the Messiah. On a mountain in front of Peter, James and John, Jesus is transfigured. He is seen in a bright light which irradiates his clothes. Moses and Elijah appear and talk with him. Then all present are wrapped in a cloud and a voice from heaven declares that Jesus is 'my Son' (Lk. 9.35).

Perhaps this is more like what the disciples had expected from a Messiah. The presence of God is very real as by his power he transcends time and death to bring Moses and Elijah to speak with Jesus. He speaks in an audible voice and uses blinding light to transfigure Jesus. Lights, voices, miracles. And Peter reacts to it by wanting to preserve the glory. The imagery of the occasion provided many allusions to the Old Testament. It was a cloud which symbolized God's leadership as it guided Israel through the wilderness wanderings and the same cloud symbolized God's presence when it rested on the Tabernacle. In addition, the Law and the Prophets, the written form of the Jewish faith, were represented by Moses and Elijah who were talking with Jesus.

Within the story there is a comment on suffering and glory. The discussion was about Jesus' 'departure which he was about to bring to fulfilment at Jerusalem' (Lk 9.31). The word used is 'exodus'—Jesus' 'going out', his 'exit'—another clear reference to the Old Testament where the word is used to designate how the Israelites left Egypt and gives its name to the second book of the Bible. However, it was this very subject—death in Jerusalem—which had caused such consternation among the disciples. Right at the very heart of this glorious event is Jesus' anticipation of his suffering. There is no getting away from it. It cannot be avoided. The devil's temptation to power without suffering and Peter's mixture of concern and affront that Jesus should even consider such an option will not deflect Jesus from his understanding of the culmination of his ministry.

A Suffering Saviour for Successful Evangelicals

How does this impact on our lives? Mainly, like Peter, we want to avoid the suffering and prolong the glory. Yet Jesus teaches that these responses are shallow and that the way to glory is through suffering. He says as much to the two disciples on the road to Emmaus after the resurrection:

> How foolish you are and slow of heart to believe all that the prophets have spoken! Did not the Christ have to suffer these things and then enter his glory? (Lk.24.25-26)

The Christian attitude to suffering is not to go looking for it as some Christians have done by wearing hair shirts and subjecting themselves to physical pain or deprivation. The world is broken enough without having to add to it; suffering will come our way soon enough. Nor should we avoid suffering, or, more likely, think that suffering is an aberration in our lives which God should not allow. Sin and suffering are two sides of the same coin. Our world is radically and comprehensively broken by sin and, if Jesus could not avoid the consequences of it in his life but faced them squarely, it is unlikely that we will in ours. We do not always realise just how profound the effects of the Fall are and in how many ways sin is at work, destroying and making wretched our emotional and intellectual environments and our ability to do anything about it. Christians experience sin as a debilitating force inside them constantly egging them on to lie, to be cruel, to be faithless, to be lazy: to feed selfishness under any guise whatsoever. The enemy does not mind whether you fill yourself up with chocolate cake or Bible studies just so long as you fill yourself up.

Most Evangelicals are aware of these forces and struggle against them as they find the new nature 'at war' with the old one, but seek gradually and persistently, with the help of the Spirit, to overcome it. But we also experience the power of sin at work in the broken world—we suffer. Some suffer to the point of death. Not many of us do but, when we do, we are surprised by suffering. Three factors operate here. Firstly, we take our bearing from the world around us which is dominated by media messages—particularly in advertising—of happy, satisfied, contented, healthy, wealthy people. So we think we should be like them because this is what 'the good life' consists of. Secondly, because of advances in medicine, most sick people we know get better. Those who are seriously ill or dying are hidden away in hospitals or hospices and unless you know someone there you can live as if such places do not exist. Even if you have had experience of them most people will change the subject rather than listen to what you know about them. Generally we expect not to get sick and, when we do, it's hard not to think that God has made a mistake. But he has not. It's just that the problems of the world are a lot deeper than we ever realised and not even clever, advanced, technologically-adept men or women like ourselves can solve them all. And it is not that God *wants* us to suffer, but he sees it as more than the catastrophe that we see. It is a catastrophe but he does not do magic to preserve Christians from it (as Superman would), he accompanies us in and through it with a love which no suffering can destroy.

The third factor that operates is that, although we see Jesus suffering, we tend to think that that is something he had to do. That was his role—to suffer *for* us. We are very well aware that he suffered in a unique way and that the result was that sin and its consequences could be eradicated altogether. By contrast, we think, our suffering is part of the problem, However, Jesus is also our example and, like us, he was at the mercy of forces which it would not have been right for him to control. He lived a righteous life which brought him into conflict with the religious and civil authorities. He was accused of crimes he did not commit and was executed after an unfair trial. He did not deserve this. It was not fair. We should not let our understanding that Christ was delivered up 'by God's set purpose and foreknowledge' (Ac. 2.23) detract from the fact that what Jesus experienced was the unfairness of his life, and at Gethsemane we see how the Calvary event itself provoked the deepest feelings of repulsion in him. He did not 'want' in any psychologically sick way to experience these things but became convinced that they could be construed as God's will. 'Not my will, but yours be done' (Lk. 22.42). Nor was there any special intervention from heaven. Golgotha is the most inglorious place imaginable—a city rubbish dump where the corpses of crucified criminals could be thrown away with the minimum fuss in the surrounding putrefaction.

The Full Extent of His Love

In Gethsemane, the events Peter had wanted not to come to pass were about to take place. Where was God now? Where were the lights, the voices, Moses and Elijah? Only the torches and voices of the arresting party and Judas leading them straight to Jesus. What should he do? If God will not intervene, Peter will. Hack about with a sword. Cut off a man's ear. The fight for the Kingdom is serious now. Let the rulers of the law take what is coming to them. The common people listen gladly to Jesus. And almost as soon as Peter has struck a blow for the Kingdom and achieved precisely the cutting off of a man's ear, the ear has been put back in place and Jesus is arrested and taken away and the disciples are scattered.

If God will not intervene. Why, we ask in our troubles, why does he not intervene? Yet, the death of Jesus of Nazareth was the most significant intervention of God in human affairs ever. The fight for the Kingdom was serious, right enough, but it was not going to be fought with swords.

During this time, Jesus felt lonely and abandoned and cried, 'My God, my God why have you forsaken me?' and when you extract the main words from this question you get the shortened form, 'Why me?', the very question we put to God in our own sufferings, the eternal cry of those powerless in the grip of suffering (Mk. 15.34). It is important to understand that Jesus has experienced this central human dilemma. It is this solidarity, rather than media illusions, which must be our starting point for many issues in the Christian life.

This vision of Jesus sees him more at the mercy of his foes than we tend to think of him. Because we have been trained to understand the events of his life as the great victory they were, we sometimes minimize the reality, extent and significance of the problems he faced. It is so important not to lose sight of that. If we lose sight of Jesus' humanity, then we lessen the extent to which he can be with us in our sufferings. Jesus himself never used his divinity in ways which exempted him from enduring to the last bitter drop the nature of the life God had granted him. Neither must we. We may not invoke his divinity in ways which dilute or mask the realities we face. He didn't.

Jesus' dilemmas were real. He had a message to communicate which was not easily grasped. He was manoeuvering among forces inimical to him. His life was a constant onslaught against physical and mental disease and distress. He taught his ideas and, after three and a half years, the culmination was not millions entering the Kingdom and missionary endeavour thriving throughout the globe—it was crucifixion. These ends were achieved through suffering—the cross was a stumbling block to the Greeks and it is to us, too, so fixated are we on unimpeded progress and success. In this world, God's glory often seems inside-out.

Towards the end of *Jesus and the Victory of God* (p. 609), N. T. Wright concludes his argument about how Jesus saw his messianic task. His picture of a man deeply versed in Scripture, committed to expressing all that he understands of God in a life of service, facing the cross as its culmination and having to rely on his faith just as we do, never fails to move me: 'At every point then, the messianic vocation to which he seems to have given allegiance led him into a dark tunnel, where the only thing left was sheer trust.'

The question that faces us is the same one as faced Peter after he had said that he did not want Jesus to suffer. At this stage in the Christian story we think Peter remarkably dim. After all it is completely obvious to us with twenty-twenty hindsight that Jesus had to suffer. Yet how different are we? We line up behind Peter and bawl in Jesus' face, 'Not me, Lord, this shall never happen to me.' And Jesus' rebuke is the same 'You want the things of men and not of God.' So who will we worship? The Jesus we want or the Jesus we've got?

The Jesus we've got does not do magic. He is not Superman. He refuses to use glory inappropriately. He will not invoke it to avoid suffering. Surprisingly there are even more important things in life than avoiding suffering. There are many occasions when, as for Jesus, it turns out that suffering is the God-honouring route. I used to think that Jesus was a Superman Jesus—although I would never have expressed it in such disrespectful terms. But essentially I just wanted Jesus to get on and fix things for me. Jesus'll-fix-it. Because Jesus chose not to exploit his unusual powers, he experienced sin and suffering and 'disarmed the powers and authorities [making] a public spectacle of them, triumphing over them by the cross' (Col. 2.15). The pattern is the same for us—suffering and then glory. And the glory that streams from Christ's victorious sufferings is eternal as Paul makes clear:

> The Spirit himself testifies with our spirit that we are God's children. Now if we are children, then we are heirs and co-heirs with Christ, if indeed we share in his sufferings in order that we share in his glory. I consider that our present sufferings are not

worth comparing with the glory that will be revealed in us. (Rom. 8.11; 16-18)

As well as hope for the future, the eternal victory over suffering brings present comfort:

Who shall separate us from the love of Christ? Shall trouble or hardship or persecution or famine or nakedness or danger or sword? As it is written: 'For your sake we face death all day long: we are considered as sheep to be slaughtered.' No, in all things we are more than conquerors through him who loved us. For I am convinced that neither death nor life, neither angels, nor demons, neither the present nor the future, nor any powers, neither height, nor depth, nor anything else in all creation, will be able to separate us from the love of God that is in Christ Jesus our Lord. (Rom. 9.35-39)

CHAPTER 5

Encounter with God

This night as I lie down to sleep
I pray the Lord my soul to keep
If I should die before I wake
I pray the Lord my soul to take.
God bless mummy and daddy
And David and Gavin
All my grannies and grampas
All my aunts and uncles
All my cousins and friends.
Keep me safe for another day
And make me a good girl
For Jesus' sake,
Amen.

As a child I was taught to say this prayer each night before I went to bed. It was my introduction to the common Christian practice of daily prayer apart from a church service. I knew that I could tell God whatever I wanted but I can't remember deviating much from the set pattern. In terms of Scripture, my experience roamed over every part of the Bible which my mother thought appropriate for me and my two younger brothers. She used children's books rather than the Bible itself but, as those books stuck pretty faithfully to Scripture and often to its words, our knowledge was accurate and detailed. While we were young and Dad was out at the Gospel meeting, she would read to us week by week. Then once we were a little older she would read to us after we all came home from the 6.30 Gospel meeting on a Sunday night. In this way we read through *Peep of Day* and *Line upon Line*—books written for Victorian Sunday schools. We also read excerpts from Hulburt's *Story of the*

Bible as well as Ladybird Bible stories and any other books that came to hand. This home learning was in addition to what we were taught at Sunday school and children's meetings, and what we picked up from Gospel and Ministry meetings. In this way my brothers and I marched through the Gospels and most of the narrative of the Old Testament—though I was always a bit shaky on the Exile. It was a startlingly good grounding in biblical knowledge which I relished. I enjoyed the stories very much and I enjoyed having them read to me—that was always a very warm and comfortable part of the week.

All these stories were very real to me, not just in the sense that I believed they were historical but also because the human perplexities and adventures seemed life-like. One of my favourite Old Testament characters was Samuel whose life as a child in the Temple I envied. I thought it would be good to be living a life where everything you did was directly serving God and you didn't have other swathes of existence which seemed not to be related to God at all. This was how I thought about my life: what happened at the meetings and through explicit religious observance was important and nothing else, whether enjoyable or boring, was as important. I also envied Samuel the experience of God speaking to him as a child which I thought would be the greatest thing that could happen to me. I also constructed a fairly detailed picture of Jesus through his actions and teaching. This was utterly invaluable as it was the rock to which I returned again and again. Whenever I came across people who thought ill of him or who said bizarre things about him, I always went back and walked through the sublime architecture of the Gospels' portrayal of Jesus.

Thus, although I do have a conversion narrative from around the age of seven, there was never a time when I did not know about Jesus or have not loved him. He was as much part of my family as all my other relations and indeed if he or Moses or Elijah had turned up in my front room my initial surprise would have been overcome with utter delight. Sometimes the stories upset me. Hulbert's *Story of the Bible* had black and white pictures of the Old Testament characters who looked like sub-Blakean figures and struck dramatic poses in order to convey emotion. I remember one picture of the Israelites in exile. I was so young I mixed it up with the Israelites who disobeyed God when Moses was on the mountain receiving the Law. The picture illustrated the verse 'By the rivers of Babylon we sat down and wept as we remembered Zion. We hung our harps on the willows.' The people looked so sad and, yes, there was a harp hanging awkwardly on a tree. This moved me to tears as I wondered why people would have disobeyed God when he had been so kind to them.

(I recently discovered that my brother had a similar experience with the same book. He cried over the story of Absalom because David had told his soldiers to be gentle with Absalom but Joab had killed him. Being allowed to read the Bible as children made very significant impressions on us, moulding us emotionally and morally into the people we were to become.)

Teenage Years and Early Adulthood

During my teens I graduated to Scripture Union notes which contained a daily Bible reading and an accompanying comment. The notes also taught me how to approach a passage of Scripture by working out what the words mean and then trying to apply them to my own life. I used these on and off into my early twenties but never really felt satisfied with them. I think one reason might have been that I usually understood the passages fairly quickly and was also usually familiar with the sorts of comments made on them. Rarely did I come across something for the first time—so thorough had my Brethren training been in the Scriptures. Part of the difficulty was that during my childhood I had often been learning at a pace that suited me but at a level of difficulty (usually in language rather than ideas) which would have been in advance of what was thought appropriate for children of my age. Thus during my teens when I was reading material suited to my age, I grew quickly bored with it because it did not present me with any sort of challenge.

This had the unfortunate effect of making me find daily prayer and Bible reading boring and it wasn't really until university that I began buying books which once again stimulated my faith and Bible reading. James Packer's *Knowing God* and John Stott's *Basic Christianity* were two of my first buys in the early 1980s and provided a great deal of help, particularly in giving me some sort of theoretical framework for understanding the faith, rather than the Brethren 'Woe is me if I preach not the Gospel' way of looking at life, universe and everything.

While it was relatively easy to keep a habit of Christian reading going—although the requisite concentration needed was not in great supply during the years when the children were babies and toddlers—prayer was another issue altogether. I had periodic bouts where I would resolve to pray every day. I would manage to keep this going for a few months and then it would dribble away again into something fairly perfunctory. There was a very frightening period after my daughter Mary was born when I couldn't pray at all and I could hardly read Scripture. Reading the Bible just made me cry. It seemed that there was a whole world inside it which I was locked out from. Or that there was a glass corridor between me and the people in the Bible and I had lost the direct access to the stories I had enjoyed in childhood. This had happened without me doing anything to provoke it that I could see—I was not aware of any egregious sin which might have caused it—but it scared me because nothing had prepared me for such a situation.

Teaching about a Quiet Time was not that frequent and on the whole it seemed to be explained as a comforting but fairly uneventful affair which kept the believer in the sunshine of God's favour. The other thing that was scary about it was that I didn't feel able to tell anyone what was happening. I had never heard of anyone who was unable to read the Bible. And though I didn't think I had done anything wrong, I wasn't strong enough to listen to someone telling me that there must be some sin somewhere or this would not be happening or giving me some other anodyne advice which didn't recognise the problem, far less go to the heart of the matter. When I prayed it was as if what secular people said was true and there was no God and the whole Christian edifice was illusory. It was during this period that I bought a book of prayers and simply read one each day praying it in so far as I felt strong enough to do so.

I now realise that at that time—in my outer life the time when the children were young followed by the onset of Neil's illness—I was pretty ill spiritually-speaking. I could only ever remember hearing one talk about spiritual illness. Adam Roxburgh of Bute Hall, Prestwick, came to Elim Hall, Kilmarnock, during my teenage years, and preached on Elijah under the juniper tree, noting as he did so the physical symptoms of Elijah's illness which were met by the angel in a physical way, 'Arise and eat, Elijah, for the journey is too great for thee' (1 Kgs 19.7). And Elijah ate and drank and slept before being able to continue. The preacher also pointed out how kind God was to him when Elijah prayed that he might die. He did not upbraid the prophet nor did he ignore the depth of his suffering. Instead he brought him freshly baked bread, cool water and allowed him to sleep. On this slight but significant memory, I discussed these symptoms not with a religious professional but my GP. The glass corridor affected everything, not just Scripture, though it was most evident there. Fortunately the GP was most sympathetic and was not surprised that looking after fairly young children, worrying about a husband with chronic fatigue syndrome and trying to manage the household with little outlet for my ridiculous mind—which was like trying to drive a Mercedes on a Scalextric track—had made things difficult for me. He encouraged me to attend editorial meetings of *Aware*—the Christian magazine which served our network of churches—which took place in London, even though I felt that I shouldn't go because the children were too young or Neil was too sick. This was advice directly opposed to the policy of co-operation with the conventional image of women propounded in our churches. It just shows what I got for worshipping images. By this time I was so tired and ragged with my circumstances that I decided to do something that I wanted to do. It seemed unbelievably selfish but I was so fed up with life as it was that it seemed the lesser of two evils.

Rocking back and forward in the sleeper berth on the way to an editorial meeting in London was like being rocked by unseen waves at the bottom of a vast dark ocean. I didn't sleep deeply because I was aware of the movement of the train but I found it oddly comforting. When I got out at Euston station I remembered that the last time I had been there myself was when I had visited a university friend who lived in Tunbridge Wells. In some ways it seemed like the last time I had been alive. The station was busy and there were all sorts of shops and all sorts of people to look at. It was engrossing.

Then I walked out into the late spring sunshine. Coming from Scotland I found it remarkably warm and, as I dislike the cold, the warmth and flowering cherries and almond blossom lightened my mood. I went in to a tiny cafe run by a Greek proprietor and had a bacon roll and a mug of tea. The man put loads of bacon inside the roll and served the tea in a huge white mug. It was like a moment out of the Narnia stories. I sat and ate and drank and began to feel almost human again. In the afternoon I went to the meeting and found it interesting. At that time we knew that *Aware* was in trouble and were trying out various strategies to save it, so the business seemed quite urgent. That evening I went to stay with the Baigents. John had given me the detailed instructions which someone like me, who has no sense of direction, actually needs if they are going to get anywhere. I remember looking on at myself, astonished, as I navigated my way through London in the warm evening on tubes and buses as if I were a part of things. Although I had ups and downs after that, the decision to go to London, which paved the way for later journeys to EA Council meetings, did mark a break with this policy of self-obliteration which I had previously been pursuing.

This more positive attitude led to me working part-time for a while at the Department of Scottish Literature in the University of Glasgow before deciding to re-train as a teacher and getting a job at St Aloysius' College as an

English teacher. This had the initial effect of ameliorating our financial circumstances. Once I had a permanent contract, I felt I had a stronger base to work from. If Neil's illness did recur then at least I was earning. This considerably reduced my anxiety levels and I enjoyed going out to work which provided a strong routine for each day and its own interests and rewards.

St Aloysius' College

However, it had a deeper impact still. For the first time in my life I had close contact with Roman Catholics. While the Brethren of my youth had no very high opinion of the Catholic Church, this was not frequently mentioned during preaching. *All* denominations fell under the stern analysis of Christendom which the Brethren had formulated and was summed up in founder J. N. Darby's phrase 'the church in ruins'. Brethren believed that denominations were so compromised that all believing people could hope to do was group together in an informal way and wait for the Second Coming of Christ which was judged to be imminent. Although some individual members did hold sectarian views, I cannot remember ever having heard these expressed in preaching. Thus I approached St Aloysius' with a great deal of curiosity as to what this group of Christians who went to separate schools in Scotland and worshipped in separate churches was like.

I greatly enjoyed what I found. In the first instance, the staff were very helpful as I made the transition from working in a university to working in a secondary school—I did not find it entirely plain sailing. The headmaster gave me time off to attend EA Council meetings. It is part of the Jesuit way that individuals are most likely to grow when they follow those instincts which God has placed in them. He was also sympathetic to the fact that I needed to take time off to attend appointments with Katie. In our target-driven society, a headmaster who is paying out a full-time salary to a member of staff, a new member of staff, a probationer, and who therefore expects a certain amount of work in return, might well be expected to be quite rigorous in the reasons he allowed staff to take time off. Adrian Porter SJ, however, was generous.

While I was settling in to a new job, I also became more aware of the Catholic, and specifically Jesuit, ethos of the school. The priests attached to the school are Jesuits but the staff belong, mainly, to Roman Catholic parishes in local dioceses. Some staff at the school are Protestants and others have no explicit faith commitment, but when employed must express a willingness to uphold the Jesuit ethos of the school. New staff attended a series of six after-school meetings to introduce them to Ignatius Loyola, the Basque Christian who was the founder of the Jesuit order. I did not find St Ignatius particularly attractive. He seemed quite a fierce individual and I found his prayer about fighting and not heeding the wounds rebarbative, as it seemed to me to sum up a sort of macho approach to faith which I had watched harden men who espoused similar thoughts. I thought it made them become unsympathetic to the suffering of others. However, being familiar with unattractive men who did great things for God in my own tradition, I was content to accept the judgement of others about him—that he was a spiritual giant—at face value and let it be. The Jesuits speak a lot about 'finding God in all things' and about becoming 'men and women for others'. As these two insights seemed to sum up important elements of the Christian faith, I hadn't the least difficulty in signing up for them.

I was very well-supported by staff, some of whom had extremely well-developed pastoral gifts. When Katie was diagnosed with chronic fatigue syndrome, the first response of one of my colleagues was to promise to pray for her, and to get her mother to pray for her too. Also other colleagues were so tuned in to my personal state that they could tell by my face whether or not I was worried. (This is perhaps not so difficult as it seems as for a number of years I think I only had two expressions—chronically worried and acutely worried.) When I reflected on this, it occurred to me that it was the same Jesus I was meeting in these people—not a different one, a 'Catholic' one, but my own Jesus whom I'd known since childhood.

It was this unmistakable recognition that enabled me to integrate spiritually with the Christians I was meeting. Although I still retain Protestant views on communion, the authority of the Pope, and have a Protestant view of the relation between the church and Scripture, I get on well with those who hold different views. There are so many things that hold us together—basic doctrine and ethics—that there is a sufficient platform for me to join in many initiatives and services. It is, of course, an abiding sorrow that I cannot take communion with my friends. It seems utterly ridiculous that anyone can stipulate that someone like me who has been steeped in the faith since conception should be barred from the table when it is obvious that Jesus Christ himself has invited and accepted me. This would have bothered me a lot more if I had had to encounter it when I was younger. Now I'm so used to churches I know doing bizarre things, I do not feel I have much room to criticise anyone else's.

I was able to offer my thoughts on how I had fitted in as a reflection at an ecumenical service convened in the school chapel and later at a school in-service day when staff were considering the topic of holiness. Before going to the school I had not realised the extent of sectarian abuse in Glasgow. Therefore for a Protestant, even such an odd Protestant as I am, to stand up and express gratitude for the pastoral care extended to me by Catholic brothers and sisters makes an impression.

So although Katie took ill at that time, there were things to be thankful for. Neil was gradually improving in health and his relapses were less severe and there were longer periods between them. Financially, things were relatively stable. My public Christian life had the stop–go character referred to earlier and my private Christian life was still mainly characterised by worry. This was fairly well-masked by a confident exterior. I knew that the Jesuits had a very developed understanding of prayer and when Damian Howard SJ, arrived at the school as the Spiritual Father, it seemed like a good time to explore this avenue.

The Spiritual Exercises

That's how I found myself in October 2001 being accepted to begin Ignatius' *Spiritual Exercises* in daily life. Ignatius believed that the spiritual capacity, like the physical body, needed to be exercised to remain healthy. Usually the *Exercises* are completed in a thirty-day retreat in a retreat house. I did not finish them until July 2002 because I was doing them as I was working; this is known as making the 'retreat in daily life'. The prayer project is divided into four sections—called 'weeks'—where one meditates on sin, following Jesus, the cross and the resurrection. I was not pinning my hopes on this. I had tried to pray in other ways and had been unsuccessful in maintaining regular habits of daily prayer. Perhaps this would help. Certainly it couldn't make me worse. And just perhaps it might deliver to me what I had always been taught to expect as the birthright of every believer—a daily, felt and real communion with God.

The *Exercises* often ask you to imagine yourself into a situation: you may be having a conversation with Christ or you might be imagining yourself into a Bible story. At first these seemed quite direct ways of putting myself into the presence of God and it was easier to imagine myself as an observer of a scene rather than part of the action. Ignatius stresses the importance of imagining the scene as fully as possible—imagining smells, sounds, the feel of textures, the look of the people and the place, the tastes of the food. To begin with this seemed to me simply like exercises in imagination and not prayer. Although it began with the prayer for a 'grace', it did not have the character of the intercessory prayer I was used to, nor, in its development, did it necessarily use the religious language of worship with which I was familiar. I did not find what I called 'imagining' very difficult, although I smiled at what my Evangelical friends would think if I told them that my spiritual work that week was to meditate on the fall of the angels.

Sin

The first 'week' was difficult because of my propensity to climb around in my own guilt. I could find no peace and often imagined myself sitting in a dark room trying to work out why God had created the world. Every time I tried to imagine God breathing into Adam's nostrils I couldn't do it. It seemed to me that there was a railway track that led from Eden to Auschwitz, that what was breathed out as divine breath in Eden was breathed in as Zyklon-B in the concentration camps, and my imagination seemed to be permanently delaying the moment that Adam would become a living being. When I began to think of sin in the dark room, the floor began to give way underneath me until I was trapped on a small shelf of earth with an abyss in front of me and various evil figures from the Old Testament baying for my blood. Eventually, at the last moment when I was about to fall into the abyss, my back was against the wall and I could do nothing to save myself, the wall behind me proved to be a tree trunk and I fell backwards into it and into safety.

What was strange about all this to me was that I discovered that what I thought were my problems were altogether other than I had conceived. My imagination, which I had had difficulty believing could be of any use in prayer, had led me to confront my true sinfulness—not the sorts of sins which Evangelicals usually impose on themselves, such as not praying enough, not loving others enough, not evangelising enough—but that area of myself in which I was twisted out of proper shape. I was finding it hard to accept that the created order was 'very good' as God had stated and I resisted salvation itself until the last possible moment. I kept trying to work out *why* the created order was good and *why* I needed salvation. This was the first time I had realised that my intellect, of which I was proud, had an engrained bias to explain and, therefore, control things. This pride was deeply inverted and presented itself, cleverly, as humility and led to the most acute mental pain as I tried to work out whether or not I was truly forgiven, what various verses meant, and how they applied to me. After the most rigorous doses of Reformed theology which dealt quite plainly with these issues, I was aghast that this unbelief was still so deeply embedded in my own psyche. So at the end of the first week there really was something to confess and receive the reassurance of forgiveness for. What was different was that this time I experienced the forgiveness as a felt reality. It did not just drop through my internal sieve where my mind accepted its reasonableness but some mechanism deeper down poured outright scorn on it and burnt it up, precipitating me back into the wearisome round of internal recriminations. This time the forgiveness seemed to stick around in a deeper, more integrated way as I began to be aware that the unyielding grip of engrained habits of perfectionism was loosening. It was an engaging beginning.

Following Jesus

Yet even at the beginning of the second week, too, my brain attempted to tie me up in knots. David Clarkson, a preacher from Glasgow, had begun his sermon one Sunday by noting how adept Christians were at deflecting God's word from their situation. This began to make me doubt my meditations on the Annunciation. When I reflected on them, I fell to analysing the practical problems Mary and Joseph faced and the problems of theodicy they presented—why would God ask Mary to accept being treated as sinful by people around her when she was innocent? Why would he ask a righteous person to appear as unrighteous even if it was to bring about the birth of the Christ?

Considering these questions made me feel cool and detached from the narrative when what I wanted was the unimpeded intimacy with Scripture that I had in childhood. This was only one of many reflections I had on the previous fortnight's prayer, but Damian picked up on it. Ignatius believed that our emotions are truer guides to our internal state than our thoughts which are so much at risk of being spin-doctored either by ourselves or others. Because for so much of the time our emotional responses appear to happen to us, rather than being willed, they are more likely to reflect accurately what is going on inside us. For a while Damian asked me to talk about my childhood and what I talked about most was my maternal grandparents' house which had a large garden. I remembered playing there with my cousins, smelling the unusual fragrance of tomato plants in my grandfather's greenhouse, playing late on summer nights with my dad and uncle until the air seemed to contain the first traces of autumn and the smoke of early bonfires drifted across the lawn. After listening to this for a while and noting the vitality of the memory, Damian said, 'So these were God's earliest words to you.' When Damian said this quietly and matter-of-factly, his words came to me with tremendous force. For if God had been speaking to me, then my life was not qualitatively different from the lives of the people in the Bible. I was very moved as I felt that God had spoken to me and I connected it too with Ian Ford's sermon the previous Sunday where he had been emphasising the fact that God often speaks in a 'still, small voice'. This was a moment of grace, first because it revolutionised my attitude to where God had been in my past and, secondly, because it was creation, which I had had so much difficulty in calling 'good', that was the medium of revelation.

Not everything came as easily. Later on in the second week, this tendency to analyse biblical passages rather than immerse myself in them reasserted itself and my prayer times were becoming longer as I attempted to master and control Scripture. (This is not to suggest that analysis of the text is wrong, it's just that when it is done in order to extend the ego illegally, it becomes counterproductive for the reader.) Damian suggested that these periods ought to be shortened. If God were going to speak he was just as capable of doing it in fifteen minutes as he was in thirty or sixty. As I left the College for Central Station just outside the Glasgow Film Theatre in Rose Street, my general mood of tranquillity evaporated and was replaced by what Ignatius calls a 'desolation'. In this mood, as opposed to the previous consolation, there is a sense of God's absence, rather than his presence which I found extremely upsetting and still do when these periods recur. I remembered Caliban's words in Shakespeare's *The Tempest*: 'When thou cams't first, thou strok'st me, made much of me...' (1.2.332). It was disorientating that God who had seemed so close and gentle had now withdrawn. It didn't seem fair. Why bring someone to a place of tranquillity and then take it away from them? Why not leave them where they were and bring those still in difficult circumstances into peace?

When Damian explained that this was a good development, I was not at all receptive to what he was saying. Ignatius' view is that desolation may occur because the Christian has sinned, or grown slack in his or her devotions, or for some other reason—often related to God's deepening work within the individual soul. He excluded the first two causes in my case—thankfully, for at that stage I still wouldn't have been able to do that myself—and then more or less said that I would just have to sit tight and wait and see what it was that God wanted to impress on me. Sitting still is not something I like doing all that much. In fact, it's because it's the opposite of 'doing' that it irritates me. I'm not that good at relaxing, preferring a change of occupation rather than a rest. This idea of doing nothing seems irresponsible in a world where so many things are crying out to be done. (And of course the subtext of all this is that as I am very good at doing them, I should be getting on with them, not sitting about waiting in the dark.) Hasn't God himself said that we are his co-workers and doesn't the apostle say that 'we should redeem the time because the days are evil' (Col. 4.5)?

However, I was to find that God was not to be bounced back into presence in my prayer life because I wanted him to. Not even if I used pious arguments. Like many Evangelicals, I am an activity junkie. Although my preferred activities are quieter than the public forms of evangelism, they are nonetheless there and deeply engrained in the fabric of my life. While God was obviously pleased with any work done in his name, it was also important for me to realise that in some ways God existed without reference to me, (although even as I write that I know that it is only a partial description of reality). God is making a personal point when something like this occurs in a person's prayer life, not writing a theological treatise, and it's often being underlined because the Christian in question needs to understand it in a deeper way than merely holding it as a theological nostrum.

After about four weeks, through close reflection on hymns which express salvation, the feeling of God's presence was again restored. This was in itself an incredible relief which also issued—ironically enough—in a period of immense energy in which I was able to write a great deal. Because of the nature of the hymns which were important to me, it clarified for me the debt I owe my own tradition *despite its popular nature.* Hymns such as 'Love lifted me', 'Safe in the arms of Jesus' and 'I love to hear the story', were part of my childhood and, although I can quite clearly see their sentimentality and 'obvious' musical nature, it is also spiritually true that within this cultural wrapper were eternal truths which I was not at liberty to disregard. I also have respect for the hymns not least because God respected them enough in the first place to use them as vehicles—no matter how bitterly criticised—for the communication of his love. The fruit of this desolation, which I had so grimly resisted, was a re-awakened sense of the scope of redemption and the amazing grace which made it possible.

However, this reawakened sense was not easily come by. I had thought that by following Jesus through the Gospels I would be on familiar ground. Instead, the experience was often one of perplexity. Often I couldn't make Jesus out. I felt as if I were tripping over my feet or that my words were coming out all wrong or that I was putting words into his mouth or that his words made no sense. For me, being a disciple was about stumbling after something only dimly perceived just as much as it was an experience of lived closeness. It was not the experience of clarity, confidence and easy faith I had thought it would be. Being with Jesus threw up as many problems as it solved.

Just as at the end of the first week, so at the end of the second, I had a renewed sense of the beauty of all God's actions which God expresses in a new way with each new day. I remember travelling into Glasgow one morning on the train in late spring. The dignified, purposeful buildings of the Glasgow skyline were bathed in beautiful pinks and golds and blues. If any other artist was going to make something as beautiful they would have announced it in advance and invited a distinguished audience. They would have tried to preserve what they had done. But this spectacular loveliness on a workaday morning which went largely unremarked seemed to me typical of the God who takes such a transforming interest in the least prepossessing of the creatures he has made. Salvation is not only functional but deeply, deeply beautiful.

Crucifixion

I was not looking forward to the 'third week' which was a sustained meditation on the crucifixion. Most Sunday morning meetings had contained such meditations and I had never felt entirely comfortable with them mainly because if it was my guilt that had caused this suffering; the enormity of the crime was so great, I couldn't live with myself. Again this was an affliction which Christian friends, with whom I had shared the difficulty, had reassured me was a disproportionate reaction to the original sin which affects all mankind. I knew myself that this was true but it seemed not to be within the power of reason to inscribe it on my consciousness. However, the 'week' was not as bad as I anticipated. I was able to observe the events of Passion Week and conclude with the rather odd—to Protestant ears—meditation of accompanying the corpse of Jesus after his burial. When I first heard this idea, I thought it was outlandish and ghoulish, but it transpired to be the first moment of peace since the previous Thursday evening and it was soothing to think that Jesus could no longer suffer any pain or torture and all the suffering was past. This was not the first time the odd-sounding things Ignatius asked the Christian to do proved to have a deep and lasting impact; I was beginning to thaw towards him. I am no longer in panicked gloom before the cross—a tremendous personal movement from fear to faith. As part of my prayer in the third week, I wrote a meditation on the crucifixion which allowed me to unite Christian Brethren traditions of Breaking of Bread worship with my developing prayer.

Resurrection

The Fourth Week of the *Exercises* focus on the Resurrection. I was really looking forward to this as I thought that it would be a glorious way to finish. Again, it didn't work out as I had thought. As I stood beside Mary Magdalene outside the empty tomb, I felt nothing but distress. The tears that I hadn't shed in the third week overtook me. Because the final prayer of the third week had been meditating on the calm after the storm of crucifixion and the fact that Jesus couldn't be hurt or humiliated any more, to come to the tomb and find no body meant that the whole cruel circus had started up again and not even his corpse was safe from his enemies. What staggered me about this was the fact that after 2,000 years of Christian history, the last forty of which I had lived through, having held the bodily resurrection of Christ as an article of faith all of my life, the resurrection of Jesus was not the first thing that came into my head when I visited the empty tomb. This difficulty in getting to grips mentally with the reality of the resurrection continued throughout the rest of the 'week'. Instead of it being the unmitigated joy and delight I had thought I would feel it was a hard road to joy, mainly because the trauma of the cross was so catastrophic, recent and painful. Sometimes I was with disciples who had heard others talking about having 'seen the Lord' and being completely non-plussed as to what to make of it. We had always thought our friends could be trusted, but these words 'seemed to [us] like nonsense (Lk. 24.11). What was being said was only part of the problem, the other thing was that it was being said in the context of the aftermath of Calvary—it somehow seemed irreverent or insane to believe. It was not until I could imagine meeting the Lord myself that my mental resistance to the whole idea of resurrection dissolved; even then it was the sensory and emotional information from the meeting which enabled my brain to loosen its tenacious hold on the idea that *human beings do not under any circumstances come back from the dead*. The meeting was not so much characterized by joy as by a deep sense of tender union and intense but wordless worship expressed so clearly in the second movement of Bach's Concerto in D minor for two violins which I was listening to at the time. So my meditations on the Resurrection were characterized by consternation, confusion and union—altogether darker than I'd anticipated. I didn't hear the high trumpet notes of joy until about a year later when I was reading about the subject.

The *Exercises* end with a prayer known as the *Contemplatio*:

> Take and receive, Lord, all my liberty, all my memory, all my understanding and my entire will. All is yours, dispose of it according to your will. Give me your love and your grace for this is sufficient for me.

In previous years the scope of the prayer, which leaves no iota of personality outside the offering, would have been too great for me to sign up to. For a long time I actively hated the hymn 'O Jesus I have promised/To serve thee to the end' because it presupposed just such a giving of oneself. I would have felt that I couldn't keep my side of the bargain and I would also have been reluctant to give up my own rights (although that's a slightly illusory concept) 'just in case'. That I was able to contemplate it all is a testament to the growth which had taken place inside me. It is also a tribute to this method of prayer that I had prayed regularly and deeply for a period of ten months. This had resulted as far as I was concerned in increasing my intimacy with God and a different sort of knowledge about myself.

Since then I have continued to use this method of prayer and have found it useful. Not only has it enabled me to pray regularly, and pray meaningfully when I pray, it has also enabled me to 'discern' where God is in relation to my daily life. In addition, it actually provokes me to do things—often things I put off doing because I felt I couldn't, or that nobody would be interested if I did—like finishing these reflections, for example.

A Companion in Prayer

It is worth highlighting again that this prayer happened in the company of another individual, skilled in prayer and personal relations. I could have come unstuck in various ways if I had tried to do it myself. It was a necessary condition that someone else listened to what I was saying about my own prayer and often put his finger on something that I didn't see the significance of. When I examined such a feature further, it often proved to be very rewarding. Although this relationship is known as spiritual direction, direction sounds a bit off-putting as if someone is telling you what to do. It's more like guidance. If you're in a situation where you don't know what to do then having someone to walk with you is incredibly helpful. From fairly near the beginning of the project, I was able to trust Damian's judgement even on the rare occasions when it conflicted with my own. It is entirely Christian that we should bear one another's burdens and so fulfil the law of Christ (Gal. 6.2).

This journey in prayer has been the single most significant advance in the Christian life I have made since leaving university. It has made me reflect on why this knowledge was not available within my own tradition. Most prayer I was familiar with was about asking God for things—usually help in situations of difficulty—but also there was intercessory prayer for the salvation of the world and the coming of the Kingdom in its fulness. It seems to me that the close relationship Evangelicals have had with God during their Quiet Time is often so intimate that they don't talk about it. It is the case that this sort of devotional life is not transmitted from one generation to the next as easily as the content of the faith and has led to this area often being neglected by young people to whom the reading it involves makes it seem off-putting.

Evangelicals do not usually have a group of people who are valued because of their maturity in prayer. During most of the *Exercises* I would see Damian for an hour a fortnight or even an hour a week during some of the more testing periods. Evangelical pastors are usually drawn to the ministry because of their attraction to preaching and they are usually very busy people. An interim report from a survey initiated by CWR Waverley Christian Counselling in association with the Evangelical Alliance conducted by the Centre for Ministry Studies at the University of Bangor, Wales, *Pastoral Care Today: Practice, Problems and Priorities in Churches Today*, showed that 90% of respondents entered the ministry/pastorate in order to preach. 88% of respondents wanted also to be a person of prayer and 86% of congregations wanted their ministers to be people of prayer. But ministers were not asked whether they regarded training others in prayer as a key part of their ministry. There is an assumption that people know how to pray, but this is not always the case. Prayer groups or prayer triplets are created in order to pray for specific things, particularly forthcoming mission activities. But a person who is available to help an individual or a group deepen personal relationships with God through prayer is not a familiar Evangelical figure. Perhaps he or she ought to be. Certainly the challenges which face Evangelicals (those daily challenges which occur in family life and church life before even considering the public challenges to faith) cannot be overcome by human activity alone, they need to be met in the strength of a prayer life which goes beyond the superficial and is in its own right one of the best blessings of the faith.

CHAPTER 6

A Grown Up Faith

One summer recently just before the school was about to re-start, I was having a look through TKMaxx in the St Enoch's Centre in Glasgow and saw a very nice red jacket which fitted me when I tried it on. Red was a bit of a departure for school clothes as I usually wear navy or grey, but to get as good a jacket as this one for a bargain price coaxed me into buying it. Red suited me.

Later that session, I was helping at a retreat based in a boarding school near Lochearnhead. On the first evening, the students were asked to look at a painting by a pupil at the school and try to imagine what the girl in the painting was feeling. Superficially the girl looked cool. She had cropped blond hair and was wearing a white tee shirt and denims. She was half-lying, half-sitting almost but not quite, looking out of the painting. She was smoking. In the background there was a red curtain. However, anything longer than the briefest of glances showed that this girl was unhappy. The expression on her face was a mixture of sadness and anger. Because the students had had to think a bit about the painting, I used it the next morning at the beginning of my talk. I was also wearing a white tee shirt and denims—as I often do—and because that fashion is so banal it did not occur to anyone that I was dressed the same way as the girl in the painting until I pointed it out. Then I talked a little about how that fashion was in many ways a disguise. It was recognisably stylish (or could be if you weren't forty, wearing jeans out of BHS and resolutely abjuring designer tee-shirts) and marked its wearer out as 'modern' and 'cool' but in fact it said very little about that person's individuality. Then I spoke a little about the red in the background of the painting picking up some of the ideas the students had associated with it: love, passion, anger, blood, life itself. I asked Alison, who was assisting me with my talk, to help me into the red jacket and explained that what I thought was going on in the painting was that the girl, in order to seem cool, was avoiding all those areas of her personality which would actually make her live instead of sitting in grumpy lassitude with all the energy of youth vitiated because she was trying to be something much less than she was, trying to be some sort of image of herself which she perhaps thought would make her more acceptable to others. Somehow she needed to integrate these hidden 'red' elements into her public 'blue' personality. I did not point out to the students how deeply personal that interpretation was.

For me the red jacket summed up the process of personal re-definition which had been taking place in me through prayer. For years the weirdness of the Brethren had left me feeling awkward about telling non-Christians about my own religious commitment. One of my most embarrassing Brethren moments was being present at an open-air meeting in a small Ayrshire mining village when I was about sixteen or seventeen. Absolutely no-one that I could see was remotely interested in the meetings we were publicising—television was much better evening entertainment and what was making me feel so bad was that I had to wear a hat. At least the men in the group looked normal if somewhat overdressed. Within the group itself, expressing feelings of embarrassment simply met with the answer that you had to be seen to be different if that was what the Gospel demanded. Well, as far as I was concerned there were no Scriptures relating to headcoverings at open airs and the only women who regularly wore hats were those over sixty or Tory councillors—pretty thin on the ground in Scottish mining villages. This wasn't suffering for the Gospel, this was having to be embarrassed because of the witlessness of others.

Obviously I shed a great deal of this natural embarrassment on contact with other Evangelicals who managed to present themselves relatively sanely when in public, allowing the focus to fall on the offence of the cross, pure and simple. Even here, though, I have never felt comfortable in evangelism because I find it hard to argue on my feet. I don't like pat answers sometimes urged on members of evangelistic teams and I'm not good at apologetics. Conclusions that I can draw after forty-eight hours' thought escape me in conversation and from that point of view I do not think I make a very credible witness. Together these two experiences have made me diffident about expressing my faith too much because it seems to me that I am not really worthy to express it.

Well, a pox on that, says the red jacket, there's more to the faith than apologetics and evangelism, narrowly defined. What my prayer indicated was that my faith was not a discrete part of myself or something that I was vaguely interested in or a sort of hobby, it actually is my life. It consumes me. It lives me. And, in turn, when I exercise it, it blazes out of me as the connection is made between the Creator and the created being who looks up to praise him. Paradoxically, it is when I am absorbed with, and, immersed in, doing this that I am most truly and deeply myself. What also surprised me was that people, unless they nursed a particular hostility to Christianity, did not reject me because of my faith. My faith was just something they associated with being me.

In the *Contemplatio*, the prayer which ends the Ignatian *Spiritual Exercises*, the believer gives to God 'all my memory', among other things. My memories of childhood have taken on a deeper significance recently. I no longer look back on them fondly merely because they were lived out in the context of a secure and extended family life but also now because it is apparent to me how truly God was present in them. The ecclesiastical context of my life could not have been greater had I been heir to that covetable Scottish description 'daughter of the manse' with its connotations of seriousness, integrity and commitment. If we weren't actually at church, we were getting ready to go or talking about what had just happened or planning what would happen or going off to support somebody else's mission.

Quite often on Sundays we would offer hospitality, either to visiting preachers and their families or to other church members. I usually helped my mum by setting the table and then, when I was older, by doing some baking. Looking back, although there was no explicit liturgy or ritual in the services I attended, by setting the table for the speakers—putting out the Harlequin cups and saucers, the extra crystal sugar and cream for the top end of the table and the silver sugar spoons, the Carlton condiment set and, on extra special occasions, mum's wedding china, and then putting them all back in their places and special boxes in the sideboard—perhaps my life was not as far removed as I had thought from that of Samuel in the Temple as I imagined him from the illustrations in the Ladybird book. And God did speak to me in those years as my prayers also helped me realise. It was purely my sense that God was only truly present in the miraculous which prevented me recognising the still, small voice which has been speaking to me all the days of my life. I now use these memories as a way of gauging my spiritual health. If I am tired I can recognise it because my present contrasts with my past. If I am OK there is equilibrium between past and present. If things are going well then elements of the goodness of the memories are developed and prolonged.

I have also made some peace with the difficulties placed on women in churches. That issue was always made more bearable because of other ways outside the local church in which it was possible to have a ministry and, of course, a great deal of the chronic pain abated on joining Seagate where it is possible to worship like a human being instead of some sort of alien half-life. Whether my gender has affected my preaching is more difficult to say. I know I get extremely bored with a lot of the preaching to which I am subjected which mainly focuses on individual piety. First, this leaves out a lot of issues which the Bible is interested in—such as peace, justice, the environment—and all of which are 'live' just now in the context of globalization. Secondly, a lot of the application of these sermons majors on 'should'—what Christians should or should not do. This is almost immediately guilt-inducing because it implies that at the moment the congregation 'is' not doing what it 'should'. Very little attention is given to how God transforms people from one to the other. To listen to preachers you get the distinct impression that we have to pull ourselves up by the bootstraps when the reality is that we are just as helpless in producing our own sanctification as we are in producing our own justification. So I like to talk more about how radical weakness provokes radical grace. The contemporary writer whom I admire and who does this best is Philip Yancey, who sums it up in the marvellous couplet which gets right to the heart of Evangelical activists' neuroses:

> Nothing I can do can make God love me any more.
> Nothing I can do can make God love me any less.

It would be very easy to 'blame' a Brethren upbringing for all of this. That would not be fair. Certainly it made it difficult for women to flourish. However, despite everything, in its backhanded way, it provided me with some excellent role models in public speaking and, through its women's meetings, even provided me with opportunities to pursue this gift. So, like the Israelites, I was able to plunder the Egyptians as I achieved my liberation. Although this seemed to be deeply frustrating, I do not feel bitter. I would not like to have to go back to a church where there was no liberty for women and it has left me exceptionally wary of any organisations and committees dominated by men. The most difficult memories to deal with are words which were spoken about biblical and contemporary women and the contempt and spite that motivated them. They don't go easily to sleep.

How this would all have played out if circumstances had been different, I don't know. Life took its own shape in the difficulties associated with my pregnancies and then Neil's and subsequently Katie's chronic fatigue syndrome, which was like walking along a mountain escarpment in the dark, putting one foot in front of another and not looking over the edge. Those circumstances provoked a searching analysis of current, popular ideas about healing which I found simply did not fit my circumstances and were the sorts of ideas that wanted to shape me into someone I was not. I was not a person without faith. I was not a person who in some perverse way unknown to me was preventing God from healing my husband. And I didn't believe in a God who deeply wanted to heal my family but couldn't because of obstacles they were raising. So I found out how God helps you to live with illness.

This experience with God made me think much more deeply about the life of Jesus and had the effect of shifting the balance of his divine and human natures, which was heavily weighted towards the divine, back towards the human. Suddenly the obstacles he faced, the risks he ran, seemed all the more real and the whole salvation project seemed all the more fragile. Much more like real life than the adventures of a sanctified Superman which I had conceived of them being before. N. T. Wright showed Jesus bringing together so many strands of Old Testament Scripture and putting them together in a radical and cutting-edge way which was not obvious to others so familiar with the same Scriptures. He did this in the context of his own faith relationship with the Father and came to the conclusion that he should offer up his life in the obnoxious form of a traitor's death. Although it seems obvious enough now, it wasn't obvious to pious Jews of the time. Jesus was living by faith. What if he wasn't right about the reading of the Scriptures? How would he cope on his own—something he'd shown anxiety about in the past? It is possible that, however Jesus faced the cross, doubts and fears were part of that process as they are part of the experience of faith. And yet he goes on, through suffering to glory and therefore he is able to sympathise completely with those flailing helplessly in the crucible of suffering and bring them to glory too.

Evangelicalism is a healthy house of faith. Within its walls, Christians can grow up, expand and develop as they grow older. I grew out of some of its more simplistic ideas while being aware of a paradox: it was within and alongside such ideas that the Word himself entered. So, did I choose the red jacket that day or did Jesus give it to me? It seemed to me, as it always does, that I chose, I decided, I acted, but when I look back it seems, too, that Jesus was there first anticipating my needs and desires before I was aware of them myself. I accept myself as the person I am and try not to waste energy on the bloodsucking 'image' that siren voices tell me would bring me popularity, wealth and happiness. Instead I find contentment in wearing the red jacket.

What will happen next I don't know. I'm not quite sure that my inner life and my outer are the best fit. The issue of vocation comes up quite often in prayer. Certainly I'd like to do more preaching and probably more writing. But it is not obvious to me at the moment that I should change direction in any radical way.

I hope these reflections have provided an insight into sanctification which is just as significant as the justification many Evangelicals write about. A Christian's life doesn't somehow sustain a conversion moment as a lifelong present. Life continues and what seemed like cast iron answers in your twenties often change and mutate in subsequent decades. This is not decline or falling away from the truth. This is normal. It is to be expected; it is growth. I have lived a very ordinary life and cannot make the claims on readers' attention which autobiography usually makes. My life is not adventurous or high-powered or famous. Even in Christian terms I cannot tell you of crowds converted or miracles accomplished. Perhaps more Christian lives are more like this than the 'signs and wonders' variety we are often oppressed by. Grown-up people need a grown-up faith which allows them to interact with God and Scripture and their circumstances in a way which does no violence to their mind, emotions and will. God will not be shoehorned into other people's understanding of him, no matter how useful it was in the past or still seems to others. He will not be contained by the best human expressions of him. He is above and beyond our ideas of him and in his huge restlessness will prod and cajole us to leave behind any expression of himself which he feels is harming us. We might find this disturbing.

But he's after us and will never allow us to settle for second best. By continuing to choose God we find we have chosen life itself in all its fulness.

At Brethren communion services in the past, it was not uncommon to hear someone pray, 'We come into thy presence, O Lord, on this the first morning of another week and here we raise our Ebenezer...' This completely incomprehensible utterance was a metaphorical reference to the Old Testament story where Samuel intercedes for Israel which has repented of its idolatry. God hears Samuel, and the Philistines who have come to attack Israel are destroyed. Samuel sets up a stone which he calls 'Ebenezer' which means 'Thus far has the Lord helped us'. Although the Brethren use of the term in the 1960s seemed to me almost as dated and eccentric as the culture to which it was meaningful in the first place, I find myself realising that the concept is useful and am grateful it is in my vocabulary, no matter in how comic a form. It is good to be able to look over a series of years and see how God has cared.

My life is utterly ordinary; his care is beyond telling.

'Thus far has the Lord helped us.' (1 Sam. 7.12)